For Yasuko

"John Dower ends this grim recounting of seventy-five years of constant war, intervention, assassination, and other crimes by calling for 'serious consideration' of why the most powerful nation in world history is so dedicated to these practices while ignoring the nature of its actions and their consequences—an injunction that could hardly be more timely or necessary as the Pentagon's 'arc of instability' expands to an 'ocean of instability' and even an 'atomic arc of instability' in Dower's perceptive reflections on today's frightening world."

—NOAM CHOMSKY

"No historian understands the human cost of war, with its paranoia, madness, and violence, as does John Dower, and in this deeply researched volume he tells how America, since the end of World War II, has turned away from its ideals and goodness to become a match setting the world on fire. George W. Bush's post-9/11 'global war on terror' was not a new adventure, but just more of the same."

—SEYMOUR HERSH

"In *The Violent American Century*, John Dower has produced a sharply eloquent account of the use of US military power since World War II. From 'hot' Cold War conflicts to drone strikes, Dower examines the machinery of American violence and its staggering toll. This is an indispensable book."

—MARILYN YOUNG

"John Dower is our most judicious guide to the dark underbelly of postwar American power in the world. Those who focus on Europe and North America speak of a Pax Americana. This is to ignore the technologies of violence that Washington meticulously deployed in Asia and the global South, from total war to 'shock and awe,' of which Dower is our unflinching analyst."

—JUAN COLE

"A lucid, convincing, and chilling account of the self-deceiving American fall into violence. Dower's clear-eyed analysis of a terrible history, for its faith in the power of truth, invites a fresh determination to demand another way. Just in time."

—JAMES CARROLL

"A timely, compact, and utterly compelling exposé of the myriad contradictions besetting US national security policy. John Dower has written a powerful book."

—ANDREW J. BACEVICH

"If you think that because we've never experienced World War III the world is becoming far more peaceful, John Dower's book is mandatory reading. In clear, carefully documented fashion, this superb historian shows just how much violence the United States has unleashed outside its borders since 1945, so much of it below the radar of our awareness at the time—and of our memories today."

—ADAM HOCHSCHILD

THE
VIOLENT
AMERICAN
CENTURY

WAR AND TERROR
SINCE WORLD WAR II

JOHN W. DOWER

Dispatch Books

Haymarket Books
Chicago, Illinois

© 2017 John W. Dower

Published by
Haymarket Books
P.O. Box 180165
Chicago, IL 60618
773-583-7884
info@haymarketbooks.org
www.haymarketbooks.org

ISBN: 978-1-60846-723-5

Trade distribution:
In the US through Consortium Book Sales and Distribution,
www.cbsd.com
In the UK, Turnaround Publisher Services,
www.turnaround-uk.com
In Canada, Publishers Group Canada, www.pgcbooks.ca
All other countries, Publishers Group Worldwide, www.pgw.com

This book was published with the generous support of the
Wallace Action Fund and Lannan Foundation.

Cover image of oil wells on fire during the 1991 Gulf War. Cover
design by Rachel Cohen.

Library of Congress CIP Data is available.

Entered into digital printing, January 2018.

CONTENTS

PREFACE

In 2015, the Japanese publisher Iwanami Shoten issued the first of a multivolume collection of topical essays on recent times, to which I contributed an article titled "War and Terror since World War II." This short book builds on that undertaking.

The subject is the same but now framed by the famous "American century" phrase coined in 1941 by publisher Henry Luce—here prefaced with the unsettling adjective "violent." Luce's resonant term caught on for obvious reasons. America did indeed emerge from the war as the most prosperous, powerful, and influential nation in the world, and it remains so today. Still, this requires many qualifications.

Despite a great deal of Pax Americana rhetoric over the course of the postwar decades, the United States never exercised anything close to global hegemony. The "Cold War" from 1945 to 1991 witnessed an alarming confrontation between the American and Soviet superpowers—or, more generally, between two "camps" or "blocs," capitalist and communist/socialist—and even this bipolar branding was a gross simplification of a fractured, tumultuous world.

Beyond this, despite the dissolution of the Soviet Union in 1991 and the consequent emergence of the United States as the world's "sole superpower," the twenty-first century has seen an ever-increasing number of reasons to dismiss the conceit of an American century. The end of the Cold War was indeed a momentous triumph for the United States, and the virtually simultaneous US demolition of Iraqi forces in the short Gulf War of 1991 seemed to confirm the nation's unassailable capabilities in a new era of digital warfare and precision weaponry. This double victory, however, turned out to be deceptive.

The United States already had experienced stalemate and defeat in Korea and Vietnam during the Cold War, despite its overwhelming power. A mere decade after 1991, military failure would prove to be the case again, as Washington's initiation of a "global war on terror" in response to al-Qaeda's attacks on the World Trade Center and Pentagon on September 11, 2001, triggered seemingly endless instability and chaos in the Greater Middle East. To Washington's enormous chagrin and frustration, the Pentagon's unprecedented technological superiority was stymied by an almost anarchic aggregation of nonstate and national actors engaged in largely low-level irregular warfare.

We are thus confronted with the contradictory picture of America as a rich and spectacularly weaponized nation of high rhetoric, enormous might, overweening hubris, profound paranoia, and deep failings and pathologies. Despite all this, the "American century" coinage still strikes me as useful. For good or ill, America bestrides the globe without truly close competitors. Its economy is second to none. Its prosperity and professed ideals are still beacons to many. However one may evaluate its success in warfighting (or peacekeeping), its reach remains impressive. The world has never seen a state with so many military garrisons in so many far-flung countries—close to eight hundred in the second decade of the twenty-first century, manned by a hundred and fifty thousand troops in around eighty nations. America's annual military-related spending is greater than much of the rest of the world combined. When it comes to maintaining and ceaselessly updating the most sophisticated instruments of destruction imaginable—and provoking allies and potential antagonists alike to try to keep pace—the United States simply has no peer.

This military preeminence, with all its fault lines and failures, is a cardinal aspect of the American century that emerged after World War II. Side by side with this—the other part of this book's title—is the violence that runs like a ground bass through these long postwar decades. Thus, one simple but central concern here has been to assemble a concise overview of the breadth, scale, and variety of global conflict and war-related death, suffering, and trauma since 1945. This extends to genocides, politicides, civil wars, and localized conflicts in which the United States may have played no role or at best a peripheral one. At the same time, America has engaged in violence abroad far more frequently than most Americans realize or perhaps care to know—sometimes in publicized deployments, sometimes in conjunction with the United Nations or the North Atlantic Treaty Organization, but frequently in solo, clandestine, and "black" operations. Both during and after the Cold War, the United States, like the Soviet Union and its successor Russia, also abetted violence through proxy wars, arms sales, and support for authoritarian regimes—all invariably undertaken in the US case in the name of peace, freedom, and democracy. A good portion of this interventionism fueled, and still fuels, anti-American blowback.

In highlighting war-related violence, I am going against a current fashion in academic studies that emphasizes the relative peacefulness of the postwar decades, even to the point of trumpeting a precipitous decline in global violence since 1945. I do not spend time directly debating the decline-of-violence apostles. They call attention to interesting quantitative trends, but I weigh the world differently—more tragically—and have attempted to show why by examining militarized violence from a range of perspectives. One focus of this scrutiny is the decades from 1945 to the collapse of the Soviet Union in 1991, where the global landscape of death and devastation makes the label "Cold War" a cruel and parochial joke.

Ever since the second year of the twenty-first century, we have lived in an age preoccupied to the point of abject fear with "terrorism," but resorting to wanton terror is hardly new. The vast scale of state terror practiced by communist nations like the Soviet Union and China under the dictatorships of Joseph Stalin and Mao Zedong, directed primarily against perceived internal enemies, left indelible stains on the reputations of such countries. Since September 11, however, terror has impinged on the consciousness of Americans, and Westerners in general, in the form of atrocious acts perpetuated largely by nonstate actors such as al-Qaeda, ISIS (Islamic State of Iraq and Syria), and their ilk. In either case, the focus is on terrorism practiced by others.

These terrorist atrocities are acknowledged in the pages that follow. At the same time, however, particular attention is given to the generally taboo subject of state terror as practiced by the United States and its allies. This includes strategic bombing from World War II through Korea in the 1950s to Southeast Asia in the 1960s and 1970s, in which densely populated cities and towns were explicitly targeted to destroy, among other things, enemy morale. Additionally, one chapter on the Cold War addresses what US strategists called "the delicate balance of terror" of the nuclear arms race, and closing sections of the book introduce the revitalization of this intimidating madness in present-day agendas for "nuclear modernization." Another chapter, on the 1980s, presents a case study of US support for right-wing Latin American regimes—and insurgent groups—engaged in "anticommunist" terror, including torture.

When the administration of George W. Bush responded to September 11 by declaring a "global war on terror" and launching the disastrous invasions of Afghanistan and Iraq, it was not really deviating from the thrust of existing policy, as so many have argued. The excessive response to the atrocity carried out by al-Qaeda's nineteen terrorists—inaugurated, in the case of the 2003 invasion of Iraq, by massive bombardment intended to "shock and awe" the foe—essentially involved unleashing a warfighting machine already primed and experienced in overseas interventions, including intensive bombing, covert operations, and practices on the "dark side."

The long endnotes to this short text can be seen, in considerable part, as a reflection of my interest in the ceaselessly evolving military technology of the American century and the insider language that accompanies this. In military parlance, as in jargon everywhere else, the language with which policies are formulated becomes quite literally formulaic (and, in the case of the military, is capped with an avalanche of acronyms). This becomes groupthink, but the group is necessarily flexible enough to rethink strategies as circumstances and technological imperatives—like the simultaneous end of the Cold War and ascendance of computerized warfare—demand. Many of the annotations call attention to insider sources where language, technology, and strategy intersect: declassified planning documents, unclassified mission statements, lower-echelon "torture manuals," think-tank studies, top-level policy pronouncements, and recollections by former strategic planners and CIA operatives who looked back on what they saw and did in the belly of the beast with critical, and sometimes scathing, second thoughts.

The endnotes also reveal my debt to the many investigative reporters who have written perceptively on the multiple tragic faces of violence of our post–World War II world. To these debts, I must add the support given to publication of this present volume by Tom Engelhardt and Nick Turse, who have set a high standard for critical reportage through their incisive writings as well as the invaluable website *TomDispatch*. Tom, a close friend since graduate school in the late 1960s, edited my final draft with generosity and occasional severity, and Dao X. Tran carefully helped smooth out lingering wrinkles as copy editor. I, of course, am responsible for all content and shortcomings.

September 30, 2016

CHAPTER 1

MEASURING VIOLENCE

We live in times of bewildering violence. In 2013, the chairman of the Joint Chiefs of Staff told a Senate committee that the world is "more dangerous than it has ever been."[1] Statisticians, however, tell a different story: that war and lethal conflict have declined steadily, significantly, even precipitously since World War II.

Much mainstream scholarship now endorses the declinists. In his influential 2011 book, *The Better Angels of Our Nature: Why Violence Has Declined*, Harvard psychologist Steven Pinker adopted the labels "the Long Peace" for the four-plus decades of the Cold War (1945–91), and "the New Peace" for the post–Cold War years to the present. In that book, as well as in post-publication articles, postings, and interviews, he has taken the doomsayers to task. The statistics suggest, he declares, that "today we may be living in the most peaceable era in our species's existence."[2]

Clearly, common sense must seek out a middle ground, acknowledging that the number and deadliness of global conflicts have indeed declined since World War II, without engaging in extravagant phrasemaking about "peace." This so-called postwar peace was, and still is, saturated in blood and wracked with suffering.

It is reasonable to argue that total war-related fatalities during those Cold War decades were lower than in the six years of World War II (1939–45) and certainly far less than the toll for the twentieth century's two world wars combined. It is also undeniable that overall death tolls have declined further since then. The five most devastating intrastate or interstate conflicts of the postwar decades—in China, Korea, Vietnam, Afghanistan, and between Iran and Iraq—took place during the Cold War. So did a majority of the most deadly politicides, or political mass killings, and genocides—in the Soviet Union, China (again), Yugoslavia, North Korea, North Vietnam, Sudan, Nigeria, Indonesia, Pakistan/Bangladesh, Ethiopia, Angola, Mozambique, and Cambodia, among other countries. The end of the Cold War certainly did not signal the end of such atrocities (as witness Rwanda, the Congo, and the implosion of Syria). As with major wars, however, the trajectory is downward.[3]

Unsurprisingly, the declinist argument celebrates the Cold War as less violent than the global conflicts that preceded it, and the decades that followed as statistically less violent than the Cold War. But what motivates the sanitizing of these years, now amounting to three-quarters of a century, with the label "peace"? The answer lies largely in fixation on major powers. The great Cold War antagonists, the United States and Soviet Union, bristling with their nuclear arsenals, never came to blows. Indeed, wars between major powers or developed states have become (in Pinker's words) "all but obsolete." There has been no World War III, nor is there likely to be.[4]

Such upbeat quantification invites complacent forms of self-congratulation. (How comparatively virtuous we mortals have become!) In the United States, where we-won-the-Cold-War sentiment still runs strong, the relative decline in global violence after 1945 is commonly attributed to the wisdom, virtue, and firepower of US "peacekeeping." In hawkish circles, nuclear deterrence—the Cold War's MAD (mutually assured destruction) doctrine that was described early on as a "delicate balance of terror"—is still canonized as an enlightened policy that prevented catastrophic global conflict.

Branding the long postwar era as an epoch of relative peace is disingenuous, and not just because it deflects attention from the significant death and agony that actually did occur and still does. It also obscures the degree to which the United States bears responsibility for contributing to, rather than impeding, militarization and mayhem after 1945. Ceaseless US-led transformations of the instruments of mass destruction—and the provocative global impact of this technological obsession—are by and large ignored. Continuities in American-style "warfighting" (a popular Pentagon word) such as heavy reliance on airpower and other forms of brute force are downplayed. So is US support for repressive foreign regimes, as well as the destabilizing impact of many of the nation's overt and covert overseas interventions. The more subtle and insidious dimension of postwar US militarization—namely, the violence done to civil society by funneling resources into a gargantuan, intrusive, and ever-expanding national security state—goes largely unaddressed in arguments fixated on numerical declines in violence since World War II.

Beyond this, trying to quantify war, conflict, and devastation poses daunting methodological challenges. Data advanced in support of the decline-of-violence argument is dense and often compelling, and derives from a range of respectable sources. Still, it must be kept in mind that the precise quantification of death and violence is almost always impossible. When a source offers fairly exact estimates of something like "war-related excess deaths," you usually are dealing with investigators deficient in humility and imagination.

Take, for example, World War II, about which countless tens of thousands of studies have been written. Estimates of total "war-related" deaths from that global conflict range from roughly fifty million to more than eighty million. (Anyone familiar with the usually well-annotated entries on wars in Wikipedia, the online encyclopedia, will recognize how regularly such discrepancies between low and high estimates of fatalities recur.) One explanation for such variation is the sheer chaos of armed violence. Another is what the counters choose to count and how they count it. Battle deaths of uniformed combatants are easiest to determine, especially on the winning side. Military bureaucrats can be relied upon to keep careful records of their own killed-in-action—but not, of course, of the enemy they kill. War-related civilian fatalities are even more difficult to assess, although—as in World War II—they commonly are far greater than deaths in combat.

Does the data source go beyond so-called battle-related collateral damage to include deaths caused by war-related famine and disease? Does it take into account deaths that may have occurred long after the conflict itself was over (as from radiation poisoning after Hiroshima and Nagasaki, or from the US use of Agent Orange in the Vietnam War)? The difficulty of assessing the toll of civil, tribal, ethnic, and religious conflicts with any exactitude is obvious. The same is true of politicides ranging from millions of mass deaths caused by government policies, deliberate or otherwise, to tens of thousands of more selective political murders by authoritarian regimes. Communist regimes account for a large percentage of these atrocities in the twentieth century, but the record of US support for brutal authoritarian governments in Latin America, Africa, Asia, and the Middle East is extensive, sordid, and (by America's own professed standards) in considerable part criminal.

Concentrating on fatalities and their averred downward trajectory also draws attention away from broader humanitarian catastrophes. In mid-2015, for instance, the Office of the United Nations High Commissioner for Refugees reported that the number of individuals "forcibly displaced worldwide as a result of persecution, conflict, generalized violence, or human rights violations" had surpassed sixty million and was the highest level recorded since World War II and its immediate aftermath. Roughly two-thirds of these men, women, and children were displaced inside their own countries. The remainder were refugees, and over half of these refugees were children.

Here, then, is a trend line intimately connected to global violence that is not heading downward. In 1996, the UN's estimate was that there were 37.3 million forcibly displaced individuals on the planet. Twenty years later, as 2015 ended, this had risen to 65.3 million—a 75 percent increase over the last two post–Cold War decades that the declinist literature refers to as the "new peace." In its report covering to the very end of 2015, the UN notes that "the global population of forcibly displaced people today is larger than the entire population of the United Kingdom."[5]

Other disasters inflicted on civilians are less visible than uprooted populations. Harsh conflict-related economic sanctions, which often cripple hygiene and health-care systems and may precipitate a sharp spike in infant mortality, usually do not find a place in itemizations of military violence. US-led UN sanctions imposed against Iraq for thirteen years beginning in 1990 in conjunction with the first Gulf War are a stark example of this. An account published in the *New York Times Magazine* in July 2003 quoted both supporters and critics of the sanctions, but accepted the fact that "at least several hundred thousand children who could reasonably have been expected to live died before their fifth birthday."[6] And after all-out wars, who counts the maimed, or the orphans and widows, or those the Japanese in the wake of World War II referred to as the "elderly orphaned"—parents bereft of their children?

Figures and tables, moreover, can only hint at the psychological and social violence suffered by combatants and noncombatants alike. It has been suggested, for instance, that one in six people in areas afflicted by war may suffer from mental disorder (as opposed to one in ten in normal times).[7] Even where American military personnel are concerned, attentiveness to trauma did not become a serious focus of concern until 1980, seven years after the US retreat from Vietnam, when post-traumatic stress disorder (PTSD) was officially recognized as a mental-health issue. In 2008, a massive sampling study of 1.64 million US troops deployed to Afghanistan and Iraq between October 2001 and October 2007 estimated "that approximately 300,000 individuals currently suffer from PTSD or major depression and that 320,000 individuals experienced a probable TBI [traumatic brain injury] during deployment." As these wars dragged on, the numbers naturally increased.[8] To humanize such disturbing data or extend its ramifications to wider circles of family and community—or, indeed, to populations traumatized by violence worldwide—defies statistical enumeration.

◆

Largely unmeasurable, too, is violence in a different register: the damage that war, conflict, militarization, and plain existential fear inflict upon civil society and democratic practice. This is true everywhere but has been especially conspicuous in the United States since Washington launched its "global war on terror" in response to al-Qaeda's attacks on the World Trade Center and the Pentagon on September 11, 2001.

Here, numbers are perversely provocative, for the lives claimed in twenty-first-century terrorist incidents can be interpreted as confirming the decline-in-violence argument. From 2000 through 2014, according to the widely cited Global Terrorism Index, "more than 61,000 incidents of terrorism claiming over 140,000 lives have been recorded." Including September 11, countries in the West experienced less than 5 percent of these incidents and 3 percent of the deaths. Another minutely documented tabulation, based on combing global media reports in many languages, puts the number of suicide bombings from 2000 through 2015 at 4,787 attacks in more than forty countries, resulting in 47,274 deaths.[9]

These atrocities are incontestably horrendous and alarming. Grim as they are, however, the numbers themselves are *comparatively* low when set against earlier conflicts. For specialists in World War II, the "140,000 lives" estimate carries an almost eerie resonance, since this is the rough figure usually accepted for the death toll from a single act of terror bombing, the atomic bomb dropped on Hiroshima. The tally is also low compared to contemporary deaths from other causes. Globally, for example, more than four hundred thousand people are murdered annually. In the United States, the danger of being killed by falling objects or lightning is at least as great as the threat from Islamist militants.[10]

This leaves us with a perplexing question: If the overall incidence of violence, including twenty-first-century terrorism, is relatively low compared to earlier global threats and conflicts, why has the United States responded by becoming an increasingly militarized, secretive, unaccountable, and intrusive "national security state"? Is it really possible that a patchwork of nonstate adversaries that do not possess massive firepower or follow traditional rules of engagement has, as the chairman of the Joint Chiefs of Staff declared in 2013, made the world more threatening than ever?

For those who do not believe this to be the case, possible explanations for the accelerating militarization of the United States come from many directions. Paranoia may be part of the American DNA—or, indeed, hardwired into the human species. Or perhaps the anticommunist hysteria of the Cold War simply metastasized into a post-9/11 pathological fear of terrorism. (Military strategists and "defense intellectuals," unnerved by the multipolar turmoil of the post–Cold War world, frequently speak almost nostalgically of the comparatively clear-cut challenges of a world in which "bipolarity" was the name of the game.) Machiavellian fear-mongering certainly enters the picture, led by conservative and neoconservative civilian and military officials of the national security state, along with opportunistic politicians and war profiteers of the usual sort. Cultural critics predictably point an accusing finger as well at the mass media's addiction to sensationalism and catastrophe, now intensified by the proliferation of digital social media.

To all this must be added the peculiar psychological burden of being a "superpower" and, from the 1990s on, the planet's "sole superpower"—a situation in which "credibility" is measured mainly in terms of massive cutting-edge military might. It may be argued that this mindset helped "contain Communism" during the Cold War and provides a sense of security to US allies. What it has not done is ensure victory in actual war, although not for want of trying. With some exceptions (Grenada, Panama, the brief 1991 Gulf War, and the Balkans), the US military has not tasted victory since World War II—Korea, Vietnam, and recent and current conflicts in the Greater Middle East being boldface examples of this failure. This, however, has had no impact on the hubris attached to superpower status. Brute force remains the ultimate measure of credibility.

The traditional American way of war has tended to emphasize the "three Ds" (defeat, destroy, devastate). Since 1996, the Pentagon's proclaimed mission is to maintain "full-spectrum dominance" in every domain (land, sea, air, space, and information) and, in practice, in every accessible part of the world. The Air Force Global Strike Command, activated in 2009 and responsible for managing two-thirds of the US nuclear arsenal, typically publicizes its readiness for "Global Strike . . . Any Target, Any Time." In 2015, the Department of Defense acknowledged maintaining 4,855 physical "sites"—meaning bases ranging in size from huge contained communities to tiny installations—of which 587 were located overseas in forty-two foreign countries. An unofficial investigation that includes small and sometimes impermanent facilities puts the number at around eight hundred bases in eighty countries. Over the course of 2015, to cite yet another example of the overwhelming nature of America's global presence, elite US special operations forces were deployed to around 150 countries, and Washington provided assistance in arming and training security forces in an even larger number of nations.[11]

America's overseas bases reflect, in part, an enduring inheritance from World War II and the Korean War. The majority of these sites are located in Germany (181), Japan (122), and South Korea (83) and were retained after their original mission of containing communism disappeared with the end of the Cold

War. Deployment of elite special operations forces is also a Cold War legacy (exemplified most famously by the army's "Green Berets" units in Vietnam) that expanded after the demise of the Soviet Union. Dispatching covert missions to three-quarters of the world's nations, however, is largely a product of the war on terror.

Many of these present-day undertakings require maintaining overseas "lily pad" facilities that are small, temporary, and unpublicized. And many, moreover, are integrated with covert CIA "black operations." Combating terror involves practicing terror—including, since 2002, an expanding campaign of targeted assassinations by unmanned drones. For the moment, this latest mode of killing remains dominated by the CIA and the US military (with the United Kingdom and Israel following some distance behind).[12]

The "delicate balance of terror" that characterized nuclear strategy during the Cold War has not disappeared. Rather, it has been reconfigured. The US and Soviet arsenals that reached a peak of insanity in the 1980s have been reduced by about two-thirds—a praiseworthy accomplishment but one that still leaves the world with around 15,400 nuclear weapons as of January 2016, 93 percent of them in US and Russian hands. Close to two thousand of the latter on each side are still actively deployed on missiles or at bases with operational forces.[13]

This downsizing, in other words, has not removed the wherewithal to destroy the earth as we know it many times over. Such destruction could come about indirectly as well as directly, with even a relatively "modest" nuclear exchange between, say, India and Pakistan triggering a cataclysmic climate shift—a "nuclear winter"—that could result in massive global starvation and death.

Nor does the fact that seven additional nations now possess nuclear weapons (and more than forty others are deemed "nuclear weapons capable") mean that "deterrence" has been enhanced. The future use of nuclear weapons, whether by deliberate decision or by accident, remains an ominous possibility. That threat is intensified by the possibility that nonstate terrorists may somehow obtain and use nuclear devices.[14]

There is little to be gained from attempting to assign responsibility for the failure to curb nuclear proliferation after Hiroshima and Nagasaki or to completely eliminate these supreme weapons of mass destruction after the collapse of the Soviet Union. What is striking at this moment in history is that paranoia couched as strategic realism continues to guide US nuclear policy—and, following America's lead, that of the other nuclear powers. As announced by the Obama administration in 2014, the potential for nuclear violence is to be "modernized." In concrete terms, this translates as a thirty-year project that will cost the United States an estimated $1 trillion (not including the usual future cost overruns for producing such weapons), perfect a new arsenal of "smart" and smaller nuclear weapons, and extensively refurbish the existing delivery "triad" of long-range manned bombers, nuclear-armed submarines, and land-based intercontinental ballistic missiles carrying nuclear warheads.[15]

Nuclear modernization, of course, is but a small portion of the full spectrum of American might—a military machine so massive that it inspired President Obama to speak with unusual emphasis in his State of the Union address in January 2016. "The United States of America is the most powerful nation on Earth," he declared. "Period. Period. It's not even close. It's not even close. It's not even close. We spend more on our military than the next eight nations combined."[16]

Official budgetary expenditures and projections provide a snapshot of this enormous military machine, but here once again numbers can be misleading. Thus, the "base budget" for defense announced in early 2016 for fiscal year 2017 amounts to roughly $600 billion, but this falls far short of what the actual outlay will be. When all other discretionary military- and defense-related costs are taken into account—nuclear maintenance and modernization, the "war budget" that pays for so-called overseas contingency operations like military engagements in the Greater Middle East, "black budgets" that fund intelligence operations by agencies including the CIA and National Security Agency, appropriations for secret high-tech military activities, "veterans affairs" costs (including disability payments), military aid to other countries, huge interest costs on the military-related part of the national debt, and so on—the actual total annual expenditure is close to $1 trillion.[17]

Such stratospheric numbers defy easy comprehension, but one does not need training in statistics to bring them closer to home. Simple arithmetic suffices. The projected bill for just the thirty-year nuclear modernization agenda comes to over $90 million a day, or almost $4 million an hour. The $1 trillion price tag for maintaining the nation's status as "the most powerful nation on Earth" for a single year amounts to roughly $2.74 billion a day, over $114 million an hour.

Creating a capacity for violence greater than the world has ever seen is costly—and remunerative.

On February 17, 1941, almost ten months before Japan's attack on Pearl Harbor, *Life* magazine carried a lengthy essay by its publisher (Henry Luce) titled "The American Century." The piece was framed as a denunciation of America's "halfway" position vis-à-vis the war then under way in Europe—the extending of aid to England while maintaining relations with Germany. The son of Presbyterian missionaries, born in China in 1898 and raised there until the age of fifteen, Luce essentially transposed the certainty of religious dogma into the certainty of a nationalistic mission couched in the name of internationalism.[18]

Isolationists who opposed US engagement in the war had many valid arguments, Luce conceded, including fear that this could accelerate "the whole trend toward collectivism" already under way in the United States and "end up in such a total national socialism that any faint semblances of our constitutional American democracy will be totally unrecognizable." Despite this fear, he insisted, isolationism was morally and politically bankrupt, a "virus" that subverted America's destiny as a beacon of "democratic idealism" and "freedom under law." Luce acknowledged that the United States could not police the whole world or attempt to impose democratic institutions on all of mankind. Nonetheless, "the world of the 20th Century, if it is to come to life in any nobility of health and vigor, must be to a significant degree an American Century." The essay called on all Americans "to accept wholeheartedly our duty and our opportunity as the most powerful and vital nation in the world and in consequence to exert upon the world the full impact of our influence, for such purposes as we see fit and by such measures as we see fit."

Japan's attack on Pearl Harbor propelled the United States wholeheartedly onto the international stage Luce believed it was destined to dominate, and the ringing title of his cri de coeur became a staple of patriotic Cold War and post–Cold War rhetoric. Central to this appeal was the affirmation of a virtuous calling. Luce's essay singled out almost every professed ideal that would become a staple of wartime and Cold War propaganda: freedom, democracy, equality of opportunity, self-reliance and independence, cooperation, justice, charity—all coupled with a vision of economic abundance inspired by "our magnificent industrial products, our technical skills." In present-day patriotic incantations, this is referred to as "American exceptionalism."

The other, harder side of America's manifest destiny was, of course, muscularity. Power. Possessing absolute and never-ending superiority in developing and deploying the world's most advanced and destructive arsenal of war. Luce did not dwell on this dimension of "internationalism" in his famous essay, but once the world war had been entered and won, he became its fervent apostle—an outspoken advocate of "liberating" China from its new communist rulers, taking over from the beleaguered French colonial military in Vietnam, turning both the Korean and Vietnam conflicts from "limited wars" into opportunities for a wider virtuous war against and in China, pursuing the rollback of the Iron Curtain with "tactical atomic weapons." At one point, Luce even mulled the possibility of "plastering Russia with 500 (or 1,000) A bombs"—a terrifying scenario, but one that the keepers of the US nuclear arsenal actually mapped out in expansive and appalling detail in the 1950s and 1960s, before Luce's death in 1967.[19]

The "American Century" catchphrase is hyperbole, of course. It has always had critics and detractors, their ranks swelling noticeably since the fiasco of the US war on terror.[20] In this critical crossfire, the slogan was never more than a myth, a fantasy, a delusion. It papered over glaring inequalities of race, class, gender, and privilege within the United States itself. Military victory in any traditional sense was largely a chimera after World War II. The so-called Pax Americana itself was riddled with conflict and oppression and egregious betrayals of the professed catechism of American values. At the same time, postwar US hegemony obviously never extended to more than a portion of the globe. Much that took place in the world, including disorder and mayhem, was beyond America's control. Yet, not unreasonably, Luce's catchphrase persists. The twenty-first-century world may be chaotic, with violence erupting from innumerable sources and causes, but the United States does remain the planet's "sole superpower." The myth of exceptionalism still holds most Americans in its thrall. US hegemony, however frayed at the edges, continues to be taken for granted in ruling circles, and not only in Washington. And Pentagon planners still emphatically define their mission as full-spectrum dominance globally. Washington's commitment to modernizing its nuclear arsenal rather than focusing on achieving the thoroughgoing abolition of nuclear weapons has proven unshakable. So has the country's almost religious devotion to leading the way in developing and deploying ever more "smart" and sophisticated conventional weapons of mass destruction.

As President Obama declared in his final State of the Union address, it's not even close. Not even close. To potential adversaries, of course, that is a provocation.

CHAPTER 2

LEGACIES OF
WORLD WAR II

Everyone agrees that World War II ended in August 1945, but when did it begin? Americans focus on the Japanese attack on Pearl Harbor in December 1941. Europeans, more reasonably, point to Nazi Germany's invasion of Poland in September 1939. If we draw a wider picture that includes Asia, the great global clash of nation-states can be said to have begun in July 1937, when Imperial Japan invaded China.

No matter where historians choose to start their story, World War II is beyond question the baseline for understanding and evaluating war and conflict in the Cold War and contemporary world. Engulfing the globe, it was the apogee of industrialized "total war," a concept that traced back to World War II. In total war, nations mobilize all the material and psychological resources of their society. At the same time, all aspects of the enemy community—including noncombatant men, women, and children—become legitimate targets.

The legacies of World War II were as immense in their cumulative and diverse ways as the war itself had been. Most immediately striking was the continuation of death, destruction, suffering, scarcity, and turbulence almost everywhere except in America. The United States emerged from the conflict with tragic but comparatively low service-related deaths: 405,399 in the official count of the US Department of Veterans Affairs, of which 291,557 were "battle deaths" and the remainder "non-theater" deaths in service.[1] The country also emerged with a populace spared invasion or enemy bombing, and with a vigorous economy that had been stimulated by war-related production. Elsewhere— in Europe, Asia, and the Soviet Union—cities lay in ruins. Uncounted millions were dead, and millions more were homeless and, indeed, often in search of new homelands. Starvation and disease were widespread, unemployment rampant, economic recovery a desperate dream. Crime and corruption flourished. Politicians in the defeated countries like Germany and Japan scurried to assume new public personas.

Another huge legacy of the war was that the erstwhile democratic victors lost their colonies, usually grudgingly and often accompanied by violence and bloodshed. Imperial Japan had invaded China (in 1937) and Southeast Asia (in concert with the attack on Pearl Harbor in December 1941) spouting noble rhetoric about creating a proud new Pan-Asianism liberated from the white man's influence and control. In practice, the Japanese were oppressive and frequently atrocious conquerors, but their routing of the colonial powers in Asia did indeed ring a death knell for colonialism. That bell tolled most dramatically for England. World War II marked the end of its reign as the empire on which "the sun never set." Rubbing salt in the wound, the United States took its place as the would-be global hegemon.

The postwar demise of Western colonial rule in Asia unfolded in a disjointed and often violent manner. The Philippines became independent in 1946, a liberation its US overlords had promised in 1916 and taken an interim step toward in 1935. India attained independence the following year, after a near century of submission to the rule of the British Raj—and then witnessed bloodshed on a massive scale as sectarian strife between Hindus and Muslims led to the shearing off of Pakistan as a separate nation. Until the end of 1949, the Dutch attempted to forcibly reimpose their rule over the "Dutch East Indies" (Indonesia), where the Japanese had briefly replaced them. In Malay (Malaysia), where a sizable population of ethnic Chinese lived alongside native Malays, the British returned at war's end to lead a ferocious counterinsurgency campaign against communist-led guerrillas comprising largely Chinese residents. The "Malay Emergency" lasted from 1948 to 1960, and Malaysia itself did not gain independence within the Commonwealth until 1957. France elbowed its way back into "French Indochina" (Vietnam, Cambodia, and Laos) and held on militarily against indigenous nationalist resistance until 1954, when the United States stepped in to take its place and lay the groundwork for the disaster later known as the Vietnam War.

World War II also bequeathed three major occupied countries (Korea from 1945 to 1948, Germany from 1945 to 1949, and Japan from 1945 to 1952), several explosively divided countries (Korea, Germany, China, and Vietnam), and ultimately a divided world. Popular use of the label "Cold War" dates from 1947, and the phrase was effective in highlighting the superpower confrontation between the United States and Soviet Union that spilled out of World War II but never quite erupted into outright war.[2] At the same time, "Cold War" also evoked the image of a bipolar world pitting a US-led capitalist sphere of influence against a Soviet-led communist bloc. This was not entirely unreasonable, as the NATO and Warsaw Pact military coalitions attest. From the outset, however, and certainly in retrospect, this rigid mindset and terminology blocked more nuanced recognition of a multitude of conflicts that were the very opposite of cold, and were frequently autonomous or indigenous in origin.

In more uplifting directions, the horrendous world war also prompted a concerted effort, led by the major victorious nations, to create global institutions that it was hoped would prevent another such conflagration. One early step in this direction was the Bretton Woods system, dating from an international conference held in New Hampshire in July 1944. The goal of the conference was to prepare the ground for orderly postwar monetary relations among nations, and its legacy was long lasting. The International Monetary Fund and International Bank for Reconstruction and Development (now expanded into the Washington-based World Bank Group) are the offspring of Bretton Woods.

The best known of the war's idealistic legacies was the United Nations, established in June 1945 to replace the ineffective League of Nations created in the wake of World War I. UN headquarters were located in New York City, as opposed to the league's Geneva home base. Among its early and most impressive accomplishments was adoption of a Universal Declaration of Human Rights in December 1948.

The war's end also witnessed the emergence of a peculiar mixture of punitive animus and idealistic aspiration in the form of pathbreaking war crimes trials. The four-nation Nuremberg Trials of German leaders (held from November 1945 until October 1946) set the pattern, and were followed by the eleven-nation International Military Tribunal for the Far East, better known as the Tokyo Trials (from June 1946 to December 1948). Judicial innovations were striking. Individual leaders were for the first time held responsible for acts of state. More sweeping yet, in addition to conventional war crimes three new criminal categories were introduced ex post facto into the trials: conspiracy to commit aggressive war, crimes against peace, and crimes against humanity (such as the murderous Nazi concentration camps).

These proceedings involved the exercise of double standards and victor's justice, even as they also reflected a remarkable infusion of genuine hope that introducing such accountability into international law would set a precedent that would go far toward inhibiting future aggression. B. V. A. Röling, the Dutch judge at the Tokyo Trials, for example, later acknowledged the "unfair features" and "grave errors" of those proceedings, but still maintained faith that the trials had contributed "to a legal development mankind urgently needed," namely, a decisive step toward "banning war and rendering it a criminal offense."[3] Such high ideals were, predictably, never realized. As it transpired, none of the victor nations sitting in judgment in those early postwar years ever seriously regarded the laws they were inventing and applying to defeated enemies as being applicable to their own countries.

Other legacies of the war are more diffuse. One such is collective memory—more specifically, the national and nationalistic war memories that never cease to influence and distort contemporary politics. Here, we enter the more esoteric terrain of mythmaking, manipulation, and the "construction" of parochial and patriotic identities.

In a different direction, World War II witnessed the genesis of new technologies of destruction that transformed the very nature of warfare itself. Best known, of course, are the atomic bombs the United States dropped on Hiroshima and Nagasaki in August

1945, but the development of nuclear weapons only highlights the remarkable breadth of technological and operational transformations that took place under mobilization for total war. The atomic bombs, for instance, were the culminating punctuation point on a revolution in airpower that included fast fighters, dive-bombers, and medium and heavy bombers carrying both powerful and incendiary explosives. These developments were accompanied by breakthroughs in radar, radio communications, bombsights, and the like, as well as by the ascendance of aircraft carriers over battleships. They also were accompanied by what one military historian has called "the supreme instrument of total war": the policy of strategic bombing. Only the United States and Britain adopted strategic bombing as a core game plan in World War II, beginning against Germany in 1942 and reaching an apex in 1945 with the US saturation bombing campaign against Japan that devastated sixty-four cities before the atomic bombs were dropped on Hiroshima and Nagasaki.[4]

Technology, technocracy, and amorality advanced hand in hand in these air operations. By the time the United States began carpet-bombing Japan, "industrial war" and psychological warfare were firmly wedded, and the destruction of enemy morale by deliberately targeting densely populated urban centers had become standard operating procedure.[5] US air forces would later carry this most brutal of inheritances from World War II to the populations of Korea and Indochina.

By war's end, napalm had been added to the list of wartime innovations. So also—although too late to be widely used—had jet aircraft and, by Germany in its death throes, the "V-1" and "V-2" rockets that would become the prototypes for postwar missiles. Major developments took place not only in other weaponry like tanks and long-range artillery, but also in medical technology, including penicillin. The first elemental modern computers were developed in England and the United States in conjunction with intelligence gathering, code breaking, and other operations. Together with this came critical early advances in information theory and automation. Alongside these technological advances, World War II also bequeathed organizational innovations and models to postwar planners by welding together the military establishment, federal agencies, universities, and the private sector. One example was the development of "operations research," in which statisticians and mathematicians were recruited to plan where, when, and how to use the new arsenals of war. A more dramatic example of public-private amalgamation was the Manhattan Project that developed the atomic bomb.

After World War II gave way to the Cold War, it became fashionable to warn of the dangers of a powerful "military-industrial complex" in America (a term usually attributed to President Dwight D. Eisenhower's farewell address in 1961). The complex was in fact more extensive than just the military and industrial sectors, but such fusion was in any case not a peculiar postwar development. It was one more carryover from the mobilization for total war.[6]

All major nations marshaled material and human resources for the war, but none did so more effectively than the United States. And only the United States—blessed by its might but also by its secure geographic location—emerged from the global conflict unscathed, apart from service-related casualties. The significance of this particular legacy cannot be overemphasized. World War II did not simply lift the United States out of the global Depression that traced back to 1929. It established it as by far the world's most prosperous nation and most advanced military power. The country's outlook was triumphal, and its confidence and self-righteousness were unsurpassed.

CHAPTER 3

COLD WAR
NUCLEAR TERROR

Triumphalism and righteousness, as it turned out, had a dark and contradictory underside: deep and abiding anxiety. This bordered on the pathological and never disappeared. The postwar American leviathan was, and has remained to the present day, essentially bipolar—hubristic and overwhelmingly powerful by all material measures, yet fearful and insecure.[1]

This was, as military planners saw it, less a handicap than a paradox to be exploited. Fear of ominous existential enemies primed the political pump to maintain support for a massive military machine. Anxiety maintained at high levels was a control mechanism that kept politicians and the public in line. It paid to exaggerate perceived threats—as, for example, the presidential campaign of John F. Kennedy did in postulating a bogus "missile gap" in the Soviet Union's favor in 1960, and the Reagan administration did vis-à-vis a disintegrating Soviet Union in the 1980s—or at least to argue for the necessity of being ever-prepared to respond to the most extreme worst-case scenarios. Careers hinged on this. So did the many public and private entities invested in "security." So did "defense"-related industrial profits.

Volatility, built into the system, was intensified by technological change as well as interservice competition for resources, especially on the part of the US Air Force. At the same time, on several occasions high-level planners even suggested that the appearance of psychological instability at the highest levels was desirable as a form of nuclear intimidation. In October 1969, during the Vietnam War, for example, the White House presided over by Richard Nixon concocted a short-lived secret plan called Operation Duck Hook in which the United States appeared to threaten Hanoi with a nuclear attack. H. R. Haldeman, one of Nixon's top aides, later quoted the president telling him, "They'll believe any threat of force that Nixon makes because it's Nixon. . . . I call it the Madman Theory, Bob. I want the North Vietnamese to believe I've reached the point where I might do *anything* to stop the war." This was neither the first nor last time that "madman" theorizing influenced nuclear planners. The line between rational and irrational war gaming was not always easy to discern.[2]

The milieu in which this mix of hubris and fear, belligerency and bluff, evolved was, of course, the long Cold War extending from 1945 to the fall of the Berlin Wall in 1989 and the collapse of the Soviet Union two years later. These were tense, genuinely perilous decades, defined in major part by the arms race that followed the Soviet test of a nuclear device in 1949. In the United States, that nuclear buildup was rationalized early on by the concept of "massive retaliation," a strategy formalized by the Eisenhower administration in October 1953 (in NSC 162/2, a National Security Council document).[3] This was followed in the 1960s by the institutionalization of a doctrine of "mutually assured destruction" that became widely known by its fittingly disturbing acronym: MAD. These doctrines all unfolded under the over-arching canon of nuclear deterrence.

In essence, massive retaliation took the World War II Anglo-American strategic practice of bombing German and Japanese cities to a new level by postulating that projected nuclear attacks should target enemy population centers. Even where military or industrial installations were primary targets, the possibility of causing staggering numbers of civilian deaths was deemed highly desirable in deterring a nuclear attack. The proclaimed goal of MAD, for example, was to have the capacity to counter a nuclear "first strike" by the enemy by launching a devastating "second strike" in response. If the enemy's strike force seemed vulnerable, however, there might even be an incentive to strike preemptively. In the often-quoted words of the influential American nuclear strategist Albert Wohlstetter, published in 1959, the US-Soviet nuclear confrontation amounted to a "delicate balance of terror."[4]

While "delicate" conveys a sense of restraint and decorum, the reality of massive retaliation was crude. This emerges with stunning concreteness in declassified top-secret documents from the early decades of nuclear planning. A June 1956 Strategic Air Command (SAC) war plan titled *Atomic Weapons Requirements Study for 1959*, for example, focused on nuclear-armed bomb-ers and the limited-range missiles then available. The study called for destroying Soviet airpower using mostly thermonuclear (hy-drogen) bombs on major military targets but also anticipated the possible necessity of "systematic destruction" of urban-industrial and "population" targets with atomic bombs.

Totaling some 800 pages, the SAC plan listed more than 1,200 potential target cities in the so-called Soviet bloc, extend-ing from East Germany to China. The total number of eligible

DGZs (Designated Ground Zeros) was roughly 3,400, including around 180 in Moscow, 145 in Leningrad, 91 in East Berlin and its suburbs, and 23 in Peking (Beijing). SAC also took this opportunity to urge adding a 60-megaton thermonuclear bomb (that is, one equivalent to 60 million tons of TNT) to its arsenal. This single weapon would have been the equivalent of over 4,000 Hiroshima bombs.[5]

In 1956, the US nuclear stockpile was in the neighborhood of 3,620 warheads, compared to 660 warheads in the Soviet arsenal. In "megatonnage," this amounted to the explosive equivalent of 9,189 million tons of TNT in the US arsenal and 360 million tons in Soviet hands. Five years later, the estimated stockpiles had grown to 22,229 US warheads (10,948 megatons) and 3,320 Soviet warheads (3,420 megatons)—an overwhelming superiority on the US side that nonetheless did nothing to dispel anxiety.[6] It was in this same year, 1961, that long-simmering tension between the United States and Soviet Union over the status of West Berlin—located in East Germany but aligned with the United States since 1948—came to a climax in a manner that brought the two superpowers to an alarming point of saber-rattling. In August, this confrontation culminated with East Germany's communist government beginning construction of the notorious Berlin Wall separating East and West Berlin.

US nuclear planners responded to the Berlin Crisis with what amounted to an update of SAC's apocalyptic 1956 study. A top-secret memorandum issued by the Joint Chiefs of Staff in June 1961 projected that if an attack were launched by all the nuclear weapons on ready alert, 199 urban and rural Soviet cities would be targeted, and projected fatalities (including from fallout) would amount to around eighty million people. If the "full force" of the nuclear arsenal were launched, it would strike 295

Soviet cities, with an estimated death toll of around 115 million. (It was not until the 1980s that scientists recognized the probability of a global "nuclear winter" arising out of climate change triggered by a nuclear war.)

As in the 1956 study, this imagined assault was not confined to the Soviet Union. The memorandum estimated that in six Soviet "satellite countries" in Europe, nuclear strikes by the US alert force would cause around 1.4 million deaths; if by the full force, fatalities would top 4 million, more than half in Poland. Although China would not test its first nuclear weapon until 1964, it was again made clear that US targeting extended to "Red China" as well. There the alert force would target 49 cities and the full force 78 cities, with projected Chinese fatalities of around 67 million and 107 million respectively.

The memo acknowledged a "general consensus" that Soviet nuclear retaliation "would leave the U.S. in a seriously damaged condition, with many millions of casualties and little immediate war supporting capability." Nonetheless, "the U.S. would continue to exist as an organized and viable nation, and ultimately would prevail, whereas the USSR would not."[7]

Apart from illuminating the hysteria that animated early planning for nuclear war, these projections are a reminder of how quickly the two atomic bombs that killed more than two hundred thousand individuals in Hiroshima and Nagasaki came to be regarded as primitive and puny. (In some circles, weapons of this size are now called "firecracker nukes.")

The explosive power of the Hiroshima bomb was equivalent to 15,000 tons of TNT, making it approximately 1,500 times more powerful than the largest conventional bomb used in World War

II. The US "Castle Bravo" thermonuclear (hydrogen bomb) test at the Bikini Atoll in 1954—which notoriously irradiated the crew of a Japanese fishing boat, one of whom died shortly thereafter—already had a yield of 15 million tons (15 megatons), a thousand times greater than the Hiroshima bomb.

SAC's desire to possess a sixty-megaton thermonuclear weapon did not materialize, but in October 1961—at the height of the Berlin Crisis—the Soviet Union tested the most powerful weapon yet detonated, a hydrogen bomb named "Tsar Bomba" with a yield equivalent to fifty megatons of TNT. This was tantamount to more than 3,300 Hiroshima bombs, and amounted to more than fifteen times the explosive power of all the bombs dropped in all of World War II.[8]

Between 1945 and 1992, the United States conducted 1,054 aboveground and underground nuclear tests and produced as many as 70,000 nuclear warheads of 65 different types. These were configured for around 115 distinct weapons systems including ballistic and cruise missiles. The counterpart figures on the Soviet side, beginning with its first test in 1949, were 715 tests and total production of around 55,000 warheads of 75 types.[9]

By the end of the Cold War in 1991, the Soviet stockpile would be, in aggregate warheads count, much larger than the US one (roughly 34,600 and 20,400 warheads, respectively). This shift in gross numbers began in the mid-1970s and reflected a growing Soviet emphasis on tactical nuclear weapons deployed in anticipation of conflict on its western front. US nuclear planners, by contrast, focused on delivering strategic warheads against the whole communist bloc. In 1989, when the Berlin Wall fell, the United States possessed an estimated 12,780 strategic warheads, as opposed to 11,529 in the Soviet stockpile. By 1991, the numbers would be 9,300 and 9,202, respectively.[10]

Beginning in the early 1960s, the United States—and sub-sequently the Soviet Union—developed a variety of short-, medium-, and long-range delivery systems. The last of these, the heart of the strategic mission, was comprised of a triad of land- and carrier-based bombers, land-based intercontinental ballistic missiles (ICBMs), and submarine-launched ballistic missiles (SLBMs). By the 1970s, both superpowers had introduced missiles with multiple warheads (MIRVs).[11]

A substantial portion of the US arsenal was deployed abroad as a key component in the "containment" of Soviet and Chinese communism. A top-secret 1978 Pentagon study declassified (with heavy redactions) in the late 1990s indicated that the United States stored thirty-eight types of nuclear weapons systems overseas in twenty-seven locations, including eighteen sovereign nations and nine former or current US territories or possessions. Those in NATO countries, first introduced in 1955, rose to 3,000 in 1960, 6,000 in 1965, and peaked at around 7,300 in 1971. Roughly half were located in Germany, which saw some twenty-one different warheads deployed on its soil.

Between 1954 and 1972, the US military stored nineteen different types of nuclear weapons on the island of Okinawa, which had remained under de facto US occupation since the end of the Pacific War in 1945. A "Pacific Ashore" table derived from the Pentagon study indicates that, from 1963 to 1970, the total number of these weapons in Okinawa was more than a thousand (peaking at 1,287 in 1967). Kadena Air Base hosted the bulk of these. Elsewhere in Japan, nuclear bombs minus their fissile cores were stored at US air bases at Misawa and Itazuke (and possibly four other bases as well), while US warships carrying nuclear weapons berthed at the great naval ports of Sasebo and Yokosuka. In late 1956, a classified report on "Atomic Operations in the Far East Command" listed thirteen separate locations in Japan used to store nuclear weapons or components, or earmarked to receive such weapons in times of crisis or war.

Other declassified documents make clear that the United States conducted planning for nuclear war in the Far East at the Fuchu and Yokota air bases outside Tokyo, as well as Kadena in Okinawa. Despite Japan's "peace constitution" and its populace's strong antinuclear sentiments as the only country on which such weapons had actually been used, in the early 1960s the Japanese Air Self-Defense Force participated in joint exercises with US forces that included procedures related to nuclear weapons. Although the United States removed most of its nuclear arsenal from Asia by the early 1970s, this did not apply to nuclear-armed warships that continued to rely on Japanese ports. In almost all of these operations, the Japanese government adopted a posture of duplicitous complicity, either denying knowledge of or ignoring such activities.

The 1950s also saw nuclear weapons deployed to Guam, Iwo Jima, Chichijima in the Bonin Islands, South Korea, Taiwan, and the Philippines. (The small islands of Chichijima and Iwo Jima remained under US military control until 1968, when they were returned to Japan.) By the end of the Eisenhower administration in 1961, it is estimated that overall Pacific-area deployments totaled upwards of 1,700 weapons. By 1963 they had grown to more than 2,300 before peaking in 1967 at more than 3,200. Most were located in Okinawa, followed by South Korea. Such weapons were withdrawn from Okinawa in 1972, when sovereignty over the prefecture reverted to Japan, from Taiwan by 1974, and from the Philippines in 1977. They remained in South Korea until 1991.[12]

Between 1946 and 1962, the United States also conducted 105 nuclear tests in the Pacific Proving Grounds, which encompassed the Marshall Islands and other mid–Pacific Ocean locations. Although these tests comprised only around 10 percent of all nuclear tests conducted by the United States, many involved highly radioactive hydrogen bombs whose explosive yield was exceptionally high. As a result, the total megaton yield of the Pacific tests far surpassed that of all other US nuclear tests combined.[13]

The prospect of ever more powerful nuclear explosions, coupled with mounting global concern about radioactive fallout, prompted conclusion of a Limited Test Ban Treaty (LTBT) in 1963. The formal, self-explanatory title of this agreement was "Treaty Banning Nuclear Weapons Tests in the Atmosphere, in Outer Space and Under Water." Negotiations were long and arduous. They dated back to 1955, the year after the "Castle Bravo" thermonuclear test at Bikini Atoll, and the final agreement was only signed in the wake of the alarming Cuban Missile Crisis of 1962, when the two superpowers came within a hairbreadth of nuclear war. The LTBT was inked in Moscow by representatives of the United States, Soviet Union, and United Kingdom, which had joined the nuclear club in 1952. France, which tested four nuclear weapons in 1960 and 1961, did not sign on until three decades later.

The ban on atmospheric and underwater tests brought an end to testing at the Pacific Proving Grounds, among other sites. Underground tests were not affected, however, and no restraints were placed on future production of nuclear warheads. As the State Department later acknowledged, the treaty "did not have much practical effect on the development and proliferation of nuclear weapons," but did establish "an important precedent for future arms control."[14]

A successful Chinese nuclear test in 1964 brought the "nuclear-weapons club" to five members. Four years later, an international "Treaty on the Non-Proliferation of Nuclear Weapons" was opened for signature, coming into force in 1970. Commonly known as the Non-Proliferation Treaty (NPT), this had several distinctive features. It sought to freeze the monopoly of the five nuclear-weapons powers. It invited other nations to pledge not to develop or otherwise obtain nuclear weapons. And it promoted the peaceful application of nuclear technology, which the nuclear-weapons club would assist others in acquiring. Both the preamble and Article 6 of the NPT expressed a commitment to pursuing in good faith the ultimate goal of "nuclear disarmament" and "a treaty on general and complete disarmament under strict and effective international control." The subsequent passage of decades showed this to be a pipe dream.

The NPT did not end the US-Soviet nuclear arms race, nor did it prevent the acquisition of nuclear weapons by other nations. By the twenty-first century, the original five nuclear-weapons states had been joined by Israel (probably in the mid-1960s, but never officially acknowledged), Pakistan and India (beginning in the 1970s, with acknowledged nuclear tests by both countries in 1998), and North Korea (from 2006). As of early 2015, 190 nations were parties to the NPL. However, three nuclear powers—Israel, Pakistan, and India—never signed the treaty, and North Korea withdrew from it in 2003.

Still, the impact of the nonproliferation ideal was substantial. Eventually, through a combination of external and domestic pressures, at least twenty-four countries that possessed nuclear weapons, or were conducting or contemplating programs to produce them, endorsed the NPT. Before 1970, this included projects under way or under consideration in Egypt, Italy, Japan, Norway, Sweden, and West Germany. After 1970, the list extended to Argentina, Australia, Brazil, Canada, Romania, South Africa, South Korea, Spain, Taiwan, and Yugoslavia. Three former Soviet republics—Belarus, Kazakhstan, and Ukraine—gave up the nuclear weapons they inherited when the USSR collapsed. In the Middle East, Iraq (in 1991) and Libya (in 2003) terminated their nuclear programs under international pressure. The reverse side of these encouraging renunciations was that promoting the "peaceful" acquisition of nuclear technology created scores of nations capable to one degree or another of turning their nuclear prowess toward weapon production should they decide to do so. As of March 2014, the Arms Control Association listed no less than forty-four such "nuclear-capable" states.[15]

The demise of the Soviet Union and end of the Cold War obviously altered the nuclear balance of terror but did not eliminate it. Politics, ideology, human nature, and technological imperatives all conspired to make that impossible, as post–Cold War developments would show.

Because these weapons of mass destruction were so frightful, there eventually developed an increasingly influential "nuclear taboo" against their use—that is, a sentiment against treating them as more or less conventional weapons that reflected not just deterrence thinking, but also a growing tide of moral opprobrium. On the one hand, fear of nuclear retaliation propelled the US-Soviet arms race to wildly irresponsible levels in the decades that followed World War II. Numerically, the combined arsenals of the two superpowers peaked at well over sixty thousand warheads in the mid-1980s. On the other hand, the runaway nature of this escalation—coupled with global grassroots movements that stressed the immoral and exceptionally abhorrent nature of these weapons of mass destruction—eventually persuaded the two countries to move, however tentatively, in the direction of nuclear arms limitation agreements. When push came to shove, it is argued, and not unreasonably, this moral condemnation played a significant role in keeping the two powers from going to war and very possibly destroying much of the world.[16]

Given what we now know from a variety of sources, however, it is also clear that good fortune and sheer luck played a major role in preventing a Cold War conflagration. While, in the end, the nuclear taboo reined in decision-makers, threats to such restraint came from three directions: the apocalyptic "holy war" mindset of the early generations of nuclear planners; human and mechanical mishaps, usually referred to as "false alarms" and "close calls," that nearly triggered accidental nuclear exchanges; and recurrent proposals by upper-level officials immune to the taboo to consider using nuclear weapons in a succession of specific post-1945 conflicts.

Two highly placed members of the Cold War nuclear community, one military and the other civilian, offer articulate examples of former nuclear warriors who eventually came out of the cold and helped pull back the curtain on the psychopathology of deterrence and "the delicate balance of terror." The military officer was General (George) Lee Butler, who ended his career as the last commander of SAC in 1991–92, followed by two years as head of Strategic Command. The civilian was William Perry, whose career as an expert on technology and weapons systems began in the late 1960s and culminated as secretary of defense from 1994 to 1997.

Butler was shocked when, upon becoming SAC commander, he saw for the first time the dense, ultrasecret, constantly updated Single Integrated Operational Plan (SIOP) that defined US nuclear policy from 1961 to 2003. His alarm intensified thereafter. Shortly after retiring, he gained domestic and international attention with a passionate mea culpa delineating his "long and arduous intellectual journey from staunch advocate of nuclear deterrence to public proponent of nuclear abolition." His twenty-seven years in nuclear policy-making, he confessed, had left him "deeply troubled."

Butler's catalog of disturbing experiences was long: investigating "a distressing array of accidents and incidents involving strategic weapons and forces"; seeing "an army of experts confounded"; confronting "the mind-numbing compression of decision-making under threat of nuclear attack"; "staggering costs"; "the relentless pressure of advancing technology"; "grotesquely destructive war plans"; and "the terror-induced anesthesia which suspended rational thought, made nuclear war thinkable and grossly excessive arsenals possible during the Cold War." In retrospect, he decried the "wantonness," "savagery," "reckless proliferation," "treacherous axioms," and voracious "appetite" of deterrence—for which he himself had helped create many systems and technologies, including "war plans with over 12,000 targets."

The collapse of the Soviet Union brought Butler enormous relief and hope—followed by alarm when it became apparent that deterrence thinking and continued faith in the desirability and inevitability of nuclear weapons remained the name of the game. "Elegant theories of deterrence," he exclaimed in one speech, "wilt in the crucible of impending nuclear war." In later recollections of the folly of deterrence, Butler pointed out that at its peak the United States "had 36,000 weapons in our active inventory," including nuclear land mines and sea mines and "warheads on artillery shells that could be launched from *jeeps*." He concluded that "mankind escaped the Cold War without a nuclear holocaust by some combination of diplomatic skill, blind luck and divine intervention, probably the latter in greatest proportion."[17]

William Perry looked back on his decades as a Pentagon consultant and official with comparable distress. He shuttled in and out of government beginning in 1967, and in a memoir titled *My Life at the Nuclear Brink*, published in 2015, heaped scorn on US nuclear policy at the height of the Cold War. Strategic thinking in the 1960s was "surreal," in Perry's view, and he found it incredible that the US Army fielded nuclear weapons "as though they were simply organic evolutions of prenuclear arms: nuclear charges for artillery pieces, nuclear charges for large bazookas . . . and nuclear charges for demolition mines." Such behavior was not just "extraordinarily reckless" but also "almost primordial." Small wonder that the Soviet Union developed tactical nuclear weapons in response, "and, in the event of war, planned to use them to destroy Western Europe's communication and political centers."

Even in the last two decades of the Cold War, when the two superpowers were attempting to negotiate bilateral arms control and reduction agreements, violence and fear hovered over the scene. "When I look back on those years," Perry recalled,

> I see a historically all-too-familiar irrational, impassioned thinking, a thinking that has led to wars throughout human history and a thinking in the nuclear age more dangerous than ever. This thinking drove the frenzied debates on nuclear strategy, drove the huge additions in destructiveness we made to our nuclear forces, and brought us to the brink of blundering into a nuclear war. It was a colossal failure of imagination not to see where this was leading. Even before

the nuclear arms buildups of the 1970s and 1980s, our nuclear forces were more than enough to blow up the world. Our deterrent forces were fearsome enough to deter any rational leader. Yet we obsessively claimed inadequacies in our nuclear forces. We fantasized about a 'window of vulnerability.' Both governments—ours and that of the Soviet Union—spread fear among our peoples. We acted as if the world had not changed with the emergence of the nuclear age, the age in which the world had changed as never before."[18]

The intellectual and organizational disarray and confusion about nuclear war that these representative documents and insider descriptions convey created the context in which mishaps occurred and bellicose planners contemplated violating the nuclear taboo. General Butler spoke vaguely of "a distressing array of accidents and incidents." William Perry described his Pentagon years as living at the nuclear brink. Military jargon even coined colorful euphemisms for nuclear accidents: "broken arrows," "bent spears," "empty quivers," the last referring to the loss of a nuclear weapon. Given the indiscriminate distribution of nuclear weapons that both men described (nuclear weapons on jeeps!), and the pervasive, irrational "rationality" that so distressed them, it is not difficult to imagine nuclear weapons accidents happening, or false alarms due to human error or mechanical glitches. But how many of these incidents were truly "close calls"?

Accidents and incidents were unquestionably rife on both sides of the nuclear confrontation, but it is the more accessible US record for which we possess most documentation. The Pentagon itself acknowledges thirty-two serious nuclear accidents, but an inside study uncovered by the investigative journalist Eric

Schlosser found that at least twelve hundred "significant" accidents and incidents occurred between 1950 and early 1968.[19] Another researcher writes in passing of US nuclear accidents falling within "a range of 43 per year to 255 per year based on classified data from 1977 to 1983."[20]

The great majority of these accidents were not remotely serious enough to bring the superpowers close to the brink. On the other hand, some were, and the freakish causes of a few close calls seem to belong in a satirical film like Stanley Kubrick's 1964 farce *Dr. Strangelove or: How I Learned to Stop Worrying and Love the Bomb*. In a jittery world of massive-retaliation groupthink, major alarms about a possible Soviet attack were triggered by a flock of birds, sunlight reflected off clouds, the rising moon, a training tape mistakenly inserted in the warning system, and a faulty computer chip costing forty-six cents. The Soviets, in turn, were at one point spooked by a Norwegian weather rocket studying the aurora borealis.

In the "empty quiver" category, in 1966 a B-52 bomber on routine nuclear patrol collided with a refueling jet over Spain, sending four hydrogen bombs plummeting to earth. While the nuclear warheads themselves did not detonate, one bomb was temporarily lost in the ocean and two exploded, contaminating the soil—and American soldiers sent to clean up the site—with plutonium radiation that was still newsworthy a half-century later.[21] Multiplied many times over, these are snapshots of the "distressing array of accidents and incidents" that prompted General Butler, and others with firsthand experience, to attribute the absence of nuclear war less to resourceful deterrence than to luck and divine intervention.

Equally unsettling is the number of Cold War conflicts in which declassified records and retrospective recollections reveal

US planners broaching first use of the nuclear option. Public as well as confidential proposals to launch a "preventive" or "pre-emptive" strike against the Soviet Union were not uncommon before the Soviets developed a serious retaliatory capability. Conflicts in which the possibility of using nuclear weapons arose include the Korean War (where General Douglas MacArthur urged using more than thirty nuclear bombs to create a radioactive belt between North Korea and China), two now-forgotten moments of tension with China in the 1950s (the "first" and "second" Taiwan Straits crises in 1954 and 1958), the Cuban Missile Crisis of 1962, the Vietnam War, and the 1991 Gulf War.

Underlying such proposals was the assumption that so alarmed William Perry: that nuclear weapons were simply the high end of conventional weaponry (one more arrow in the quiver, as the saying went), and could be used *tactically.* In the acronym-saturated world of military planning, tactical nuclear weapons joined the jumble as TNW, close kin to theater nuclear forces or TNF. In 1966, as the United States ramped up its military operations in Vietnam, the Pentagon supported a study of the feasibility of using TNWs. Directed by prominent scientists including Steven Weinberg and Freeman Dyson, a secret report on the subject—*Tactical Nuclear Weapons in Southeast Asia*—reaffirmed the nuclear taboo.[22]

None of this prevented hard-line nuclear planners from continuing to assert the usefulness of such weapons in combat situations, even after the Cold War ended. By this time, of course, the number of "nuclear-weapons nations" had expanded to include countries regarded as less organizationally stable than the United States.

CHAPTER 4

COLD WAR WARS

"Total war" may have disappeared after 1945, but preparations for it did not, nor did the unleashing of massive brute force short of nuclear weapons or the decimation of civilian populations. During the Korean War (1950–53)—where the United States and the Republic of Korea (South Korea) confronted enemy forces from the People's Republic of China as well as the Democratic People's Republic of Korea (North Korea)—the tonnage of bombs dropped by US forces was more than four times greater than had been dropped on Japan in 1945. General Curtis LeMay, who directed the strategic bombing of both Japan and Korea, later observed, "We burned down just about every city in North and South Korea both. . . . We killed off over a million civilian Koreans and drove several million more from their homes, with the inevitable additional tragedies bound to ensue."[1]

In the Vietnam War between 1965 and 1973, an intense US bombing campaign that eventually extended to Cambodia and Laos dropped more than forty times the tonnage of bombs used on Japan. The secret bombing of Cambodia in 1970 offers a glimpse into the American mindset in these furious "limited wars," promoted by both civilian and military leaders. In a now-declassified document, Henry Kissinger, then serving as national security adviser to Richard Nixon, conveyed a presidential order to the air force in these terse words: "A massive bombing campaign in Cambodia. Anything that flies on anything that moves." As the critic Tom Engelhardt has observed, this is about as close as one can get to damning evidence of culpability for a war crime.[2]

Unrestrained devastation took place on all sides in the Korean and Vietnamese conflicts. In addition to intensive bombing, US forces in Vietnam also resorted to chemical warfare in the form of herbicides aimed at destroying crops and defoliating the natural coverage that enemy forces were exploiting. This, too, had roots in World War II, when American and British scientists collaborated in developing the strain of herbicides that later became notorious as "Agent Orange" for projected use against Japanese rice crops in 1946 (by which time the war had ended). This chemical weapon became available for use in Korea just before the end of hostilities in 1953 and was used by the British to destroy crops during the Malayan Emergency that dragged on to 1960. Between 1962 and 1971, under the code name Operation Ranch Hand, the US military sprayed around twenty million gallons of Agent Orange over parts of Vietnam, Cambodia, and Laos. In addition to laying waste to agricultural and forested land, this use of toxic chemicals also caused grievous human damage, including malnutrition and starvation, miscarriages, birth defects, and a range of long-term health problems including cancer.[3]

Where the postwar exercise of military force by the Soviet Union is concerned, after installing puppet regimes in Eastern Europe (Poland, Hungary, Romania, Bulgaria, Czechoslovakia, and East Germany) beginning in 1944, the most flagrant Soviet military interventions of the early Cold War era were directed at crushing popular protests in East Germany in 1953, Hungary in 1956, and Czechoslovakia in 1968. In 1969, Sino-Soviet confrontation over border issues that had simmered through the 1960s culminated in short-lived but alarming hostilities. None of these operations involved conspicuously high casualties, however, or with a few exceptions are generally regarded as wars per se.[4]

The major Soviet military engagement during the Cold War took place in Afghanistan from the closing days of 1979 to early 1989 and essentially rang the death knell for the Soviet Union, which dissolved two years later. This war, which involved Soviet intervention and occupation in support of an unpopular communist Afghan government, was condemned by Muslim nations as well as the General Assembly of the United Nations. It also attracted US, Saudi Arabian, and Pakistani support for anti-Soviet Islamist mujahedeen (guerrillas engaged in holy war) within Afghanistan, as well as other Islamic holy warriors who joined them from as many as forty countries. This, as it transpired, was the seedbed out of which Islamist terrorism against Americans and other foreigners emerged in later decades.[5]

While war convulsed Afghanistan, it also ravaged nearby Iraq and Iran, which engaged in a savage confrontation that lasted from 1980 until 1988 and included Iraqi use of chemical weapons against both combatants and civilians. The Soviet Union offered grudging support to both sides in this conflict, but especially to Iraq. The United States backed Iraq both openly and covertly in a variety of ways, including economic aid, military satellite intelligence, arms sales, and sales of dual-use technology and chemical and biological pathogens.[6]

As always, it is impossible to give precise estimates of the human costs of these Cold War wars. In the Korean War, total deaths of all combatants (notably Chinese, North Korean, and South Korean soldiers, plus a comparatively small number of US and UN battle fatalities) may have been in the neighborhood of eight hundred thousand, and the civilian death toll in North and South Korea combined possibly double that number. Some sources place these figures considerably higher. Where Vietnam is concerned, in 1995 the country's communist government estimated that two million civilians and 1.1 million communist combatants from both the North Vietnamese Army and the Viet Cong insurgents in the South were killed between 1955 and 1975. When estimated deaths of 300,000 South Vietnamese Army personnel are added to this, the possible death toll on the Vietnamese side comes to 3.4 million. On the US side, as of 2015, the Vietnam Veterans Memorial in Washington, DC, listed 58,307 names, of which around 1,200 were identified as missing in action and presumed dead. Military losses in the Soviet-Afghanistan war, including mujahedeen, almost certainly totaled over 100,000, and civilian fatalities may have ranged from as many as 850,000 to almost twice that number. Many millions of Afghans—possibly up to one-third of the nation's population—fled the country, and perhaps two million more were displaced within it. In the Iran-Iraq War, estimates of the death toll range from official figures of 250,000 Iraqis and 155,000 Iranians to more than one million.[7]

◆

The Korean, Vietnam, and Soviet-Afghanistan wars were to greater or lesser degrees "proxy wars," in which the Cold War ideological clash of communism and anticommunism was conspicuous. At the same time, they also were indigenous civil conflicts compounded by foreign intrusion. China's intervention in the Korean War in October 1950, when US forces appeared to threaten its border, provides an illustration of the multifaceted nature of war and conflict after World War II. It was only one year earlier that Mao Zedong's communist forces had consolidated their victory in China over Chiang Kai-shek's routed Nationalist forces, after four years of bloody civil war that claimed at least a million lives—by some estimates, many more.[8]

China's plight can be seen as mirroring the labyrinthine nature of World War II and its legacies. In China itself, Japanese aggression paved the way for communism's victory. In Asia more generally, Japan's failed war delivered a fatal blow to British, Dutch, and French colonialism, leaving behind a legacy of bitterly contested civil conflict and anti-imperialist wars of liberation. The Korean War itself arose out of deep domestic schisms that traced back to Japan's era of colonial rule from 1910 to 1945—schisms exacerbated by the decision of the victorious Allied powers to divide the country into Soviet and US zones at the thirty-eighth parallel in 1945.

Under the canopy of "Allied powers" versus "Axis powers" and nation-states battling nation-states, a great range of subsidiary conflicts took place in the course of World War II that in one way or another carried over into the postwar world. Civil wars festered beneath the veneer of wartime unity. Discord between erstwhile allies was rife, most conspicuously between the Soviet Union and United States. In both the European and Asian theaters, irregular paramilitary and guerrilla warfare complemented the clash of huge mechanized forces. Anticolonial movements gathered strength—a premonition of the "wars of national liberation" that would roil Asia and Africa in the postwar years. Atrocities were ubiquitous, and massacres unexceptional. The Nazi Holocaust foreshadowed a postwar world in which genocides and other mass murders would continue to occur with appalling frequency.[9]

A compilation funded by the CIA and titled "Major Episodes of Political Violence," for example, itemizes 331 episodes of "international, civil, ethnic, communal, and genocidal violence and warfare" between 1946 and 2013 in which more than five hundred fatalities have been recorded. Of this total, 222 occurred before 1990. Excluded from the tabulation were "the much larger numbers of persons directly and indirectly, physically and psychologically, distorted and disturbed by violence during episodes of armed conflict (for this we have no estimation procedure)."[10]

Even with such constraints, the compilation's death estimates are grim. In roughly chronological order, they include 500,000 killed in the struggle for independence against the French in Indochina between 1945 and 1955; one million dead in the partition of India and Pakistan between 1946 and 1948; 250,000 fatalities in "La Violencia" in Colombia between 1948 and 1960; 100,000 battle-related deaths in Algeria's struggle for independence from France between 1954 and 1962; 500,000 dead in ethnic warfare in Sudan between 1956 and 1972; 100,000 killed in ethnic warfare in Zaire between 1960 and 1965; 150,000 Kurds killed in Iraq between 1961 and 1993; 500,000 alleged communists, many of Chinese ethnicity, slaughtered by the government in Indonesia in 1965 and 1966; 200,000 dead in ethnic strife in Nigeria between 1966 and 1970; around 500,000 Chinese killed in the Cultural Revolution between 1966 and 1975; 150,000 indigenous peoples murdered in Guatemala between 1966 and 1996; a million fatalities in the ethnic war between Pakistan and Bangladesh in 1971; 250,000 killed in ethnic warfare in Uganda between 1971 and 1978; 750,000 Eritreans and others killed in ethnic warfare in Ethiopia between 1974 and 1991; 1.5 million Cambodians exterminated by the genocidal Khmer Rouge in Cambodia between 1975 and 1978; 1 million dead in the civil war in Angola that began in 1975 and continued to 2002; 180,000 killed by the Indonesian government in the "colonial war" in East Timor between 1976 and 1992; 500,000 civil war fatalities in Mozambique between 1981 and 1992; and one million killed in renewed ethnic war in Sudan between 1983 and 2002.

Other episodes of tragic mass violence can be added to this sample list, and the rounded-off numbers are open to challenge. The sweep and intensity of suffering, however, especially in what used to be called the third world, is clear. Other well-known databases offer different but similarly grim enumerations. The Correlates of War (COW) Project, for example, catalogs deaths in formal conflicts beginning in 1816, with the fatality baseline being a thousand battle deaths. For the period between 1945 and 2007, COW itemizes 242 wars and concludes that "over two million battle deaths have occurred worldwide in nearly every decade since World War II."[11] Data covering 1946 through 2013 compiled by the Uppsala Conflict Data Program (UCDP) in Sweden records "254 armed conflicts (114 wars)" between 1946 and 2013. Of this total, 110 armed conflicts (67 wars) took place before 1989, and 144 armed conflicts (47 wars) after that.[12]

The United States had little or no impact on many of these conflicts but major influence on more than a few of them. Between 1946 and the end of the twentieth century, the US military participated unilaterally or headed coalition forces in roughly a dozen operations apart from Korea and Vietnam that are commonly categorized as wars. These include Lebanon (1958); Cuba (the abortive 1961 "Bay of Pigs" invasion); the Dominican Republic (1965–66); Bolivia (1966–67); Lebanon again (1982–83); Grenada (1983); Panama (1989–90); the Gulf War (1991); the "no-fly zone" over Iraq (1991–2003); Somalia (1992–93); Haiti (1994–95); Bosnia (1994–95); and Kosovo (1998–99).

More wide-ranging compilations, including government reports, itemize "hundreds of instances in which the United States has used its armed forces abroad in situations of military conflict or potential conflict or for other than normal peacetime purposes." Many of these interventions involved multinational missions endorsed by the United Nations or NATO. Many were dispatched in the name of promoting democracy or providing humanitarian relief. Some were responses to invitations from foreign governments or undertaken to protect or evacuate US nationals believed to be in threatening situations. A small number involved responses to provocative anti-American incidents.[13]

Even establishment sources acknowledge many of these operations were ineffective or contributed to reactionary and repressive developments in the targeted countries, and this is just the tip of the iceberg. In practice, led primarily by the CIA, the United States also conducted hundreds of interventions that were covert, clandestine, or at best attracted little if any sustained attention outside the locales where they occurred. These secret actions took place beneath the radar of conventional number crunching. Technically, the formal distinction between "covert" and "clandestine" operations is that the former hides the identity of, or permits "plausible denial" by, the operation's sponsor, while the latter seeks to conceal the operation itself. In practice, this distinction is commonly blurred and these operations and their perpetrators—however criminal their activity, and however thoroughly they may become exposed—are never held accountable.

Exposés of such activities have come from testimony by former CIA whistle-blowers, sporadic congressional investigation of certain targeted transgressions, and dogged investigative journalism. One carefully documented source, for example, now itemizes eighty-one major US "covert operations" between 1945 and the collapse of the Soviet Union in 1991.[14] Cumulatively, such revelations add up to a dossier of egregious and immoral behavior of the sort true believers in the virtue of the American Cold War mission commonly associate with fascist or communist oppression. This is grist for the cottage industry of cynical espionage thrillers that have gained postwar and contemporary popularity in print and film. To the foreign nations, communities, groups, families, and individuals targeted over the long Cold War and post–Cold War decades, however, it is not fiction.

The roots of these activities trace back to the CIA's World War II precursor, the Office of Strategic Services (OSS), whose objective was to crush enemies and destabilize governments and societies deemed hostile. One mundane illustration of this lineage is a 1944 OSS classified booklet titled *Simple Sabotage Field Manual*, written primarily with operations in Europe in mind. This was essentially updated and circulated by the CIA in the 1980s in the form of an illustrated English and Spanish pamphlet aimed at destabilizing Nicaragua, then under a left-wing government.[15]

In practice, CIA activities directed at sabotage, destabilization, and the repression or destruction of communist, socialist, and progressive movements, mostly in the third world, were anything but simple. Operations on the dark side included carrying out or abetting assassinations; supporting right-wing dictators and death squads; sponsoring or supporting coups in such countries as Iran, Guatemala, Syria, Iraq, South Vietnam, Chile, and Indonesia; training and assisting foreign police in repressive and criminal tactics (in Cambodia, Colombia, Ecuador, El Salvador, Guatemala, Iran, Iraq, Laos, Peru, the Philippines, South Korea, South Vietnam, and Thailand, among other places); recruiting white Europeans and South Africans to fight in African countries like Angola and the Congo; trafficking in drugs and weapons (to help support covert activities); operating secret prisons; engaging directly and indirectly in murder, torture, terror bombing, and economic sabotage; promoting disinformation; creating and funding ostensibly "liberal" academic and political front organizations; and corrupting ostensibly democratic elections (even in major countries like Japan and Italy) by funneling money to favored conservative and right-wing candidates or parties.

One notorious CIA project code-named MKUltra, which functioned from the early 1950s to 1973, engaged scores of American institutions including universities and hospitals in secret "mind-control" experiments aimed at enhancing torture and interrogation. Other projects, most notoriously Operation Chaos, targeted domestic dissent in the United States, especially but not exclusively during the Vietnam War, in the 1960s and 1970s. The rationale in the latter case was that such protest movements reflected foreign influence.[16]

In 1987, an organization founded by more than a dozen disillusioned former CIA officials issued a statement denouncing "U.S. covert operations that killed, wounded and terrorized millions of people whose countries were not at war with the United States, nor possessed the capabilities to do remarkable physical hurt to the United States, who themselves bore the United States no ill will nor cared greatly about the issues of 'communism' or 'capitalism.'" Without providing concrete details, these contrite ex-operatives concluded "at least six million people have died as a consequence of U.S. covert operations since World War II."[17]

◆

Several developments in the final decade of the Cold War lifted the US military and paramilitary presence abroad to quantitatively and qualitatively new levels. One was the introduction of presidential policies known as the "Carter Doctrine" (in 1980) and "Reagan Doctrine" (from 1981 to 1989), which redefined strategic targets and missions. Another was intensification of CIA-led covert and clandestine activities in the Western hemisphere as well as the Middle East, involving the established tactics of infiltration, subversion, torture, and terror. Yet another late–Cold War development was the adaptation of digital and other advanced technologies to weapons systems and military command structures, captured in the phrase "revolution in military affairs." Policy and technology came together dramatically in 1990–1991, when the Iraqi dictator Saddam Hussein invaded Kuwait and triggered the Gulf War at the very moment the Soviet Union was dissolving.

The Carter Doctrine took its name from President Jimmy Carter, and was a response to two events that had their genesis in 1979: the Islamic Revolution that overthrew Washington's client regime in Iran, and Soviet military intervention in Afghanistan. The common concern in both could be summarized in a word: oil. On January 23, 1980, in the last State of the Union address of his presidency, Carter emphasized three international challenges: Soviet projection of power beyond its borders, "the overwhelming dependence of the Western democracies on oil supplies from the Middle East," and turbulent change in the developing world "exemplified by the revolution in Iran."[18]

Although Carter failed in his bid for a second term as president, his "doctrine" laid the ground for an enhanced US infrastructure of war, especially in the Greater Middle East. Less than two months after his address, Carter oversaw creation of a Rapid Deployment Joint Task Force that tapped all four major branches of the military (army, navy, air force, and marines). Within two years, this evolved into Central Command (CENTCOM), responsible for operations in Southwest Asia, Central Asia, and the Persian Gulf. At the same time, the US naval presence was extended in the Persian Gulf and Indian Ocean, initiating what one official navy historian called "a period of expansion unmatched in the postwar era."[19] Simultaneously, Carter's national security adviser Zbigniew Brzezinski launched the effective but ultimately nearsighted policy of providing support to the Afghan mujahedeen combating Soviet forces in their country. Conducted mainly through the CIA, the objective of this top-secret operation was, in Brzezinski's words, "to make the Soviets bleed for as much and as long as is possible."[20]

Carter's successor Ronald Reagan inherited these initiatives and ran with them, even while belittling his predecessor's policies. In his presidential campaign, Reagan promised "to unite people of every background and faith in a great crusade to restore the America of our dreams." This, he went on—in words that surely pleased the ghost of Henry Luce—necessitated repudiating policies that had left the nation's defense "in shambles," and doing "a better job of exporting Americanism."

One of Reagan's ringing campaign slogans was the need to exorcise "the Vietnam syndrome" that made Americans regard that recent war as if "we were the aggressors bent on imperialistic conquests." The war had been "in truth, a noble cause," he declared, and the syndrome was in fact created by the "North Vietnamese aggressors," whose goal "was to win in the field of propaganda here in America what they could not win on the field of battle in Vietnam." Reagan denounced arms-control negotiations that allowed the Soviet Union to engage in "a one-sided nuclear arms buildup," raised alarm at a world in which "the Soviets and their friends" were advancing "in the face of declining American power," and pledged to restore "the means and the determination to prevail" if forced to fight.[21] After winning the presidency, his administration also lost little time discarding Carter's tentative attempts to introduce human rights as a genuine standard in the conduct of foreign policy. That the Soviet Union had just invaded Afghanistan certainly enhanced the persuasiveness of accusations of communist expansionism. As president, Reagan moved decisively to implement his campaign promises. He set his sights on the creation of a six-hundred-ship navy, and came close to achieving this (there were 591 warships in 1989 when he left office). By 1987, the annual defense budget was roughly 40 percent larger than in 1980, and the weapons procurement budget within it had doubled. Major new weapons went into production in these years, including precision-guided munitions and stealth capabilities central to the revolution in military affairs.[22] 1987 also saw creation of a unified Special Operations Command (SOCOM) to coordinate covert and clandestine operations by special forces representing all branches of the armed services.

Under the Reagan Doctrine, the CIA stepped up its covert operations. Support for Afghan insurgents was elevated to one of the agency's most protracted interventions, code-named Operation Cyclone and conducted largely through Pakistan's secretive Inter-Services Intelligence agency. Complemented by aid from Saudi Arabia, Britain, Egypt, and China (the "Sino-Soviet split" was ongoing), this took the form of financial support, training, and weapons. Between 1986 and 1988, the weaponry included possibly as many as 2,300 US-supplied advanced shoulder-fired surface-to-air Stinger missiles to be used against Soviet helicopters, jets, and transport planes.[23]

Nor did the Reagan administration waste time before symbolically exorcising the Vietnam syndrome. In the fall of 1983, under the code name Operation Urgent Fury, it launched an invasion of Grenada, an island micro-nation in the Caribbean with a population of around 91,000 that was embroiled in political disorder involving left-wing factions. The US invasion force numbered around 7,300 troops, composed largely of rapid-deployment special units from the four military services (a preview of later more formal arrangements under the Special Operations Command).

Hostilities lasted from October 25 to December 15. On November 2, the General Assembly of the United Nations, by a vote of 108 to 9, condemned the invasion as "a flagrant violation of international law." US losses came to nineteen killed and nine helicopters destroyed. Fatalities on the other side are estimated to have been less than a hundred, including forty-five Grenadian military personnel, twenty-five Cuban paramilitaries, and at least twenty-four civilians, of whom eighteen were killed in the accidental bombing of a mental hospital. The military subsequently awarded more than five thousand medals for merit and valor to participants in Operation Urgent Fury.

Coming in the wake of a "no win" war in Korea, a humiliating defeat in Vietnam, the shocking Islamic revolution in Iran, and a terrorist suicide attack that killed 241 American marines in a barracks in Beirut, Lebanon, only two days before the invasion, this miniscule victory prompted the president to exult: "Our military forces are back on their feet and standing tall." This made for a front-page headline in the *New York Times*.[24]

More sustained and lethal than Operation Urgent Fury was the new administration's commitment to standing tall throughout Latin America. This entailed jettisoning human rights concerns and intensifying overt and covert "anticommunist" activity there—a case study in proxy war and surrogate terror that invites a chapter of its own.

CHAPTER 5

PROXY WAR
AND SURROGATE TERROR

The long and generally shameful history of US overt and covert interventions in South and Central America traces back to the turn of the twentieth century. Before World War II, these incursions, commonly in defense of US business interests, even involved protracted military occupations of Nicaragua (1912–33) and Haiti (1915–34). During the Cold War, intervention was more covert, but just as unrelenting. John Coatsworth, a distinguished scholar of Latin American economic and international history, calculates that between 1948 and 1990 the US government "secured the overthrow of at least twenty-four governments in Latin America, four by direct use of US military forces, three by means of CIA-managed revolts or assassinations, and seventeen by encouraging local military and political forces to intervene without direct US participation, usually through military coups d'état."[1]

Notorious among these postwar intrusions was the overthrow of democratically elected governments in Guatemala (1954), Brazil (1964), and Chile (1973). Nothing, however, obsessed North Americans looking south more than the political event Washington was unable to manipulate: the Cuban revolution that deposed the dictator Fulgencio Batista in the opening days of 1959. This Marxist revolution in the Caribbean was compounded by the alarming nuclear missile crisis of 1962, when the United States discovered Soviet missiles being installed in Cuba. From then on, planners in Washington and their right-wing allies throughout Latin America used the rationale of "preventing another Cuba" to justify clamping down on dissident domestic movements across the board, from militant Marxist agitators to socialists and liberals to anyone critical of the status quo or engaged in working to alleviate misery among the rural and urban poor.

A mid-1960s US congressional investigation reported having "found concrete evidence of at least eight plots involving the CIA to assassinate [Cuban leader] Fidel Castro from 1960 to 1965."[2] This was grist for cloak-and-dagger media reports. More difficult to grasp, or even see, was the sustained manner in which police states south of the border secretly coordinated their crackdowns on critics of all stripes, invariably in the name of anticommunism and invariably with the support of the United States.

A decisive step in this support took place in 1963, when the administration of President John F. Kennedy tasked the army's School of the Americas (SOA), established in 1946 and initially located in Panama under a different name, with training South and Central American military officers and police in counterintelligence and counterinsurgency. The SOA's classes were conducted mostly in Spanish. By the end of the century, the school had trained around fifty-five thousand officers plus roughly four thousand police and civilians from some twenty-two or twenty-three countries. A striking number of its graduates were to become prominent leaders in the "dirty wars" that would ravage Argentina, Chile, Colombia, Guatemala, Peru, El Salvador, Ecuador, Honduras, Panama, and Nicaragua. Along the way, the SOA acquired such derisive sobriquets as School of Assassins, School of Dictators, School of Coups.[3] Taking sides in dirty wars was typical of the proxy conflicts that engaged the United States and Soviet Union worldwide and shredded the so-called Long Peace of the Cold War. In Latin America, this mostly involved the United States extending funding, training, organizational and operational advice, weapons, logistical intelligence, and the like to authoritarian regimes engaged in "countersubversive" activities, as well as to right-wing movements dedicated to subverting reformist and left-wing governments. Washington thus found itself supporting state terror on the one hand and violence and terror against the state on the other.

The top-secret South American transnational campaign of state-sponsored terror known as Operation Condor was a beneficiary of covert US support of the former sort. Dating from the late 1960s and formally consolidated in 1975, Condor involved collaborative cross-border intelligence, apprehension, abduction, rendition, interrogation, torture, assassination, and extrajudiciary execution operations among dictatorial regimes in the "Southern Cone" nations of Argentina, Chile, Uruguay, Brazil, Paraguay, and Bolivia, later joined by Ecuador and Peru. Upwards of fifty thousand to sixty thousand individuals appear to have been killed or "disappeared" in Condor-directed actions in the 1970s and 1980s, with countless thousands imprisoned and, in many cases, tortured. More than a few victims were exiles who had fled their native countries and were engaging in human rights campaigns as refugees.[4]

The targets of this collaborative state terror extended beyond armed militants and avowed Marxists to include anyone associated with criticizing the existing right-wing regimes or advocating social justice. This was spelled out not just in the back rooms of ruling juntas, but also in training provided by the CIA and SOA. We have a clearer picture of this tutelage from instructional materials disclosed over the course of the 1980s and 1990s that became collectively identified in the media as "torture manuals."

In these dense manuals, many of them translated into Spanish, "insurgent" and "guerrilla" were the words commonly used to stigmatize critics or dissidents. *Terrorism and the Urban Guerrilla*, a teaching guide introduced to SOA classes in Spanish in 1987, expresses this succinctly: "Examples of hostile organizations or groups are paramilitary groups, labor unions, and dissident groups." Another SOA manual, *Handling of Sources*, is even more expansive: "The CI [counterintelligence] agent should consider all organizations as possible guerrilla sympathizers. . . . By infiltrating informants in the diverse youth, workers, political, business, social and charitable organizations, we can identify the organizations that include guerrillas among their members." Elsewhere in the instructional guides the identification of explicit targets is extended to refugees, political parties, peasant organizations, intellectuals, teachers and students, universities, priests and nuns, and so on. One appalling quotation translated from a torture manual identifies target groups as "religious workers, labor organizers, student groups, and others in sympathy with the cause of the poor."[5]

Upon assuming power in 1981, the Reagan administration stepped into this violent world with unrestrained ardor and callous indifference to actual conditions on the ground. Despite much evidence to the contrary, the enemy was reaffirmed to be monolithic communism, directed from Moscow and spearheaded by its Cuban apprentice. As 1980s policymakers saw it, the threat was especially dire in Central America. Guatemala, where brutal repression had taken place ever since the CIA coup in 1954, was subjected to continued special attention. El Salvador and Nicaragua also became targets of fervent counterinsurgency—and insurgency—campaigns. In El Salvador, the "anticommunist" agenda involved supporting a dictatorial regime against any and all opponents. In Nicaragua, the situation was reversed. There, the Reagan administration devoted almost evangelical energy to nurturing and supporting the Contras, a terrorist "guerrilla" campaign against the left-wing Sandinista government that in 1979, with considerable popular support, had overthrown the brutal, US-supported Somoza family dictatorship that dated back to 1936.

Disclosure of classified texts and other disturbing information pertinent to covert US activity in Central America took place sporadically but frequently between the mid-1980s and mid-1990s. Much of this focused on the sensational (and farcical) Reagan-era "Iran-Contra" scandal that broke open in 1986 and involved a convoluted plot to obtain funds for the right-wing insurgents in Nicaragua by using Israel as an intermediary to sell weapons to fundamentalist and anti-American Iran for use in its war with Iraq (to which the United States was also providing support). The less remembered CIA and SOA written materials that surfaced during these years existed at a low level in the hierarchy of covert activity and were not policy documents, but for good reason they also caused a stir. They provide a glimpse into the mindset behind anticommunist covert activities, and a graphic case study of what "exporting Americanism" in this last decade of the Cold War involved at ground level.

The first significant instructional manual to come to public attention was a guide in Spanish prepared by the CIA for the Contras. Titled *Psychological Operations in Guerrilla Warfare* in the original English draft, this eighty-nine-page text was greeted with shock in the United States when exposed by journalists in 1984. After introducing it as "a primer on insurgency, a how-to book in the struggle for hearts and minds," for example, *Time* magazine went on to observe: "Some of the 'techniques of persuasion' are benign: helping the peasants harvest crops, learn to read, improve hygiene. Others are decidedly brutal: assassination, kidnaping, blackmail, mob violence. It could be a manual for the Viet Cong or the Cuban-backed rebels in El Salvador. If it were, the Administration would likely be waving it as proof of the thesis about the sources of insidious world terrorism."[6]

Complementing *Psychological Operations* and also exposed in 1984 was another CIA Spanish-language project: a cartoon booklet airdropped into Nicaragua. Titled (in the English translation) *The Freedom Fighter's Manual*, this was as crude and pedestrian as *Psychological Operations* was vicious, but still disturbing in its own way as an exercise in low-level terrorist activity. It instructed citizens in scores of acts of vandalism (cutting cables, sabotaging machinery, putting dirt or water in gasoline tanks, setting fires, freeing farm animals, and so on) that might help bring the left-wing Sandinista government to its knees.[7]

The torture manuals, which came to belated public attention in the 1990s, consisted of seven Spanish-language SOA texts, totaling 1,169 pages. These were distributed to military officers in eleven South and Central American countries between 1987 and 1991 and also used by instructors in School of the Americas classes. The manuals reflected teaching materials used since 1982, when the Reagan administration dismissed the human rights concerns tentatively initiated during the Carter presidency. These SOA resources were complemented by two CIA "counterintelligence" manuals—one recycled from 1963, and one dated 1983 that essentially replicated this.[8]

While the torture manuals open a small window onto Washington's pervasive disregard for democracy, human rights, and the rule of law when it came to covert activities, they also cast light in other directions. One is the care taken to ensure a measure of plausible deniability about what was really being promoted. Rhetorically, this was done with euphemisms and genuflections to propriety: death squads were referred to as "Freedom Commandos" and "Freedom Fighters," for example, and slogans like fighting for "God, Homeland, and Democracy" were promoted. Procedurally, a measure of plausible deniability was obtained by directing CIA and SOA activity largely to pedagogy rather than actual hands-on violence—without calling attention to the fact that this involved teaching right-wing military, paramilitary, and police forces how to most efficiently engage in infiltration, interrogation, torture, terror, and "neutralization" of perceived enemies.

Once these various manuals became public, Washington's predictable machinery of "public diplomacy" went into motion. The SOA teaching guides were declared "inconsistent with U.S. policy." The school's course offerings also were said to include respect for human rights. "Objectionable and questionable" passages amounted to no more than two dozen—and in any case were nothing more than a "mistake" made by some misguided junior officer working from "outdated intelligence materials." Problematic statements had "escaped oversight." "A few bad apples" were involved in promoting, or practicing, torture. And in any case, excesses had been "corrected."[9]

This was, as all spin is, disingenuous. The manuals were indeed wordy—they are numbing to read—but what SOA teachers emphasized and their students found most engaging was precisely what caused these materials to be called torture manuals.

This was confirmed by Major Joseph Blair, a covert operative who (like remorseful members of the nuclear priesthood and repentant tell-all CIA agents) ultimately came in from the cold. Blair had held a responsible position administering the CIA-led Phoenix assassination program during the Vietnam War, and in the early 1980s had moved on to the SOA, where he assisted the creator of the controversial manuals in the classroom. Interviewed in 1997, after having retired in 1989, he described "primarily using manuals which we used during the Vietnam War in our intelligence-gathering techniques. The techniques included murder, assassination, torture, extortion, false imprisonment."

Turning to the argument that objectionable passages were but a miniscule part of the 1,100-plus pages of SOA instructional materials, Blair pointed out that "the officers who ran the intelligence courses used lesson plans that included the worst materials contained in the seven manuals. Now they say that there were only eighteen to twenty passages in those manuals in clear violations of US law. In fact, those same passages were at the heart of the intelligence instruction." As for the claim that SOA instructors took care to teach human rights, he noted that this amounted to a few hours and was roundly regarded by instructors and students alike as a joke.[10]

As Blair observed, much of what the CIA and SOA disseminated in the way of "counterintelligence" and "counterinsurgency" teachings was essentially repackaged from materials the agency had developed in the 1950s and 1960s. Its 1963 manual—titled *KUBARK Counterintelligence Interrogation* (KUBARK was code for CIA)—runs to 128 typescript pages and reads like a graduate-school thesis. Replete with a lengthy annotated bibliography, it summarizes the latest findings in psychological and psychiatric literature on how to exploit human vulnerabilities most effectively, through noncoercion if possible and coercion if necessary. (In its peculiar way, this scholarly veneer reflects yet another World War II legacy: the mobilization for war of "applied" social sciences.)[11]

Both *KUBARK* and its 1983 update—titled *Human Resource Exploitation Training Manual*—contain lengthy chapters devoted to "non-coercive" and "coercive" counterintelligence techniques. The 1963 text succinctly summarizes the subjects addressed under the latter category as follows: "arrest, detention, deprivation of sensory stimuli through solitary confinement or similar methods, threat and fear, debility, pain, heightened suggestibility and hypnosis, narcosis [use of drugs], and induced regression."

This catalog and the ensuing discussion of coercive techniques is repeated in the 1983 update, along with almost everything else that appears in the 1960s urtext. For anyone interested in original documents, however, the copy of the 1983 update the Defense Department eventually declassified presents an unusual feature: It is full of handwritten corrections that spotlight egregious passages while leaving the original text completely legible. The doctored declassified text also includes a new prefatory page titled "Prohibition Against Use of Force," stating that "the use of force, mental torture, threats, insults, or exposure to unpleasant and inhumane treatment of any kind as an aid to interrogation" is illegal and often counterproductive. Instruction in these techniques then duly follows.

Many of the corrections are perversely entertaining. In its opening pages, for example, the original 1983 text reads: "While we do not stress the use of coercive techniques, we do want to make you aware of them and the proper way to use them." The penciledin revision changes this to: "While we deplore the use of coercive techniques, we do want to make you aware of them so that you may avoid them." Similarly, "Coercive 'Questioning' Techniques," a section title, is revised to read "Coercive 'Questioning' Techniques and why they should not be used."

When the cosmetic changes are ignored, as anyone confronted with the corrected text could (and predictably would) do, the techniques of interrogation that carried over from the 1960s to the 1980s are plain to see. Scattered throughout the 1963 and 1983 manuals is advice about blindfolding and handcuffing seized individuals, stripping them naked, and subjecting them to an examination "including all body cavities"; garbing them in ill-fitting prison clothes; holding them incommunicado; threatening to harm their families; depriving them of food, sleep, and access to toilets; subjecting them to extremes of heat, cold, and moisture; holding them in solitary confinement, sometimes "in a cell which has no light"; forcing them to stand at attention for long periods; and so forth. Even the original 1963 manual, however, takes care to note that excessive reliance on debility, pain, et cetera can be counterproductive and result in false confessions.

The 1963 manual emphasizes that interrogators must obtain higher-level authorization "if bodily harm is to be inflicted," or "if medical, chemical, or electrical methods or materials are to be used to induce acquiescence," or "if the detention is locally illegal" or could be traced back to the CIA. More practically, it advises, "the electric current should be known in advance, so that transformers and other modifying devices will be on hand if needed." (In 1981, an Uruguayan intelligence officer reported that training manuals he had seen listed some thirty-five nerve points where electrodes could be applied during electroshock torture. Another SOA graduate from earlier years recalled attending classes where "people from the streets" were brought in and an American physician dressed in green fatigues gave instruction about "the nerve endings of the body" and demonstrated "where to torture, where and where not, where you wouldn't kill the individual.")[12]

KUBARK and its 1983 offspring *Human Resource Exploita-*
tion, like the SOA manuals used between 1982 and 1991, were
exercises in how to identify, detain, interrogate, and deter critics
of Washington's police-state allies south of the border. By contrast, in *Psychological Operations in Guerrilla Warfare,* the CIA
manual written for the Contras and brought to public attention
in 1984, it is guerrillas and insurgents who are being instructed.
Section titles alone give a sense of what was taught: "Implicit and
Explicit Terror," for example, and "Selective Use of Violence for
Propagandistic Effects."

"An armed guerrilla force can occupy an entire town or small
city that is neutral or relatively passive in the conflict," the text
explains at one point. This force should then proceed to destroy
military and police installations, cut communications, set up am-
bushes, and "kidnap" all government officials and agents. "As a
general rule," this passage continues, "the Armed Propaganda
teams should avoid participating in combat. However, if this is
not possible, they should react as a guerrilla unit with tactics of
'hit and run,' causing the enemy the greatest amount of casualties with aggressive assault fire, recovering enemy weapons and
withdrawing rapidly."

At one point, *Psychological Operations in Guerrilla Warfare*
calls for emulating Nazi "fifth column" tactics used at the start
of World War II, whereby infiltration and subversion prepared
the ground for Germany's invasions of Poland, Belgium, Holland,
France, and Norway. Where necessary, the advice continues,
"professional criminals" should be hired to carry out "specific
selected 'jobs.'" On other occasions, it might be desirable to
provoke confrontations that will "create a 'martyr' for the cause."
At "mass concentrations and meetings," the Contras are advised
to bring "Shock Troops. These men should be equipped with

weapons (knives, razors, chains, clubs, bludgeons) and should march slightly behind the innocent and gullible participants."

◆

Where the torture manuals refer to "neutralizing" targets, this was commonly recognized as a euphemism for killing. There is no evidence that covert US forces participated directly in the grotesque torture, death squads, massacres, and "disappearances" characteristic of the dirty wars that ravaged Latin America, only that they promoted and supported them. At the same time, there is little or no evidence that, in taking sides in these wars and training and materially aiding "anticommunist" participants in them, the United States gave serious attention to human rights or the rule of law. In most countries south of the border, Washington supported right-wing regimes in their state terror. In Nicaragua, it abetted the Contras in pursuing a murderous campaign of "guerrilla" terror against the government. Proxy war, surrogate terror, disdain for human rights and even for plain decency all came together.

As always, it is not possible to quantify the costs of this violence with any exactitude. For South and Central American societies, the political, cultural, and psychological costs were—and to some degree still are—enormous. Writing in the *Cambridge History of the Cold War*, John Coatsworth observed that the Contra insurrection in Nicaragua devastated the economy, forced the government to abandon most of its social programs, and "cost the lives of 30,000 Nicaraguans, mostly civilian supporters of the Sandinista revolution." He put the death toll in El Salvador between 1979 and 1984 at nearly forty thousand, most of whom were unarmed combatants murdered by the armed forces.

Coatsworth also notes in passing that President Reagan visited Guatemala City in December 1982 and praised the ruling military junta for its commitment to defend the country against the threat of communism. In 1982–1983 alone, that government forced eight hundred thousand peasants into "civil patrols" ordered to uncover and kill insurgents or see their communities destroyed. It followed up on its threat by destroying an estimated 686 villages and hamlets and killing between fifty thousand and seventy-five thousand people.

All told, Coatsworth estimates that the Cold War in Central America saw nearly three hundred thousand deaths in a population of thirty million, plus a million refugees who fled the area, mostly for the United States. Based on examination of published CIA and State Department materials plus other reports unsympathetic to communist regimes, he reached this conclusion: "Between 1960, by which time the Soviets had dismantled Stalin's gulags, and the Soviet collapse in 1990, the numbers of political prisoners, torture victims, and executions of nonviolent political dissenters in Latin America vastly exceeded those in the Soviet Union and its East European satellites. In other words, from 1960 to 1990, the Soviet bloc as a whole was less repressive, measured in terms of human victims, than many individual Latin American countries."[13]

This does not diminish the multiple horrors of Soviet violence and oppression, but helps place them in perspective.

CHAPTER 6

NEW AND OLD
WORLD ORDERS: THE 1990s

The United States entered the last decade of the twentieth century on a wave of confidence and celebration not seen since 1945. The collapse of the Soviet Union, which left America as the world's "sole superpower," was a prime reason for this. This triumph coincided, moreover, with two other interrelated developments that contributed to the celebratory atmosphere.

One was spectacular victory in the short Gulf War of 1991, in which a multination force led by the United States crushed Iraq's armed forces with negligible casualties on the coalition side. In sharp contrast to Grenada seven years earlier, this was a major military undertaking. Washington led the largest international coalition since World War II, composed of thirty-four nations including many Arab states. In this clash of nations, massive forces were mobilized on both sides: close to seven hundred thousand coalition troops (more than half a million of them American) versus several hundred thousand Iraqis.

The coalition victory was one-sided to an extreme. After a five-and-a-half-month buildup of forces in and around Saudi Arabia, the actual military campaign, called Operation Desert Storm, lasted a mere forty-three days, from January 17 to February 28. US-led coalition air forces pounded the country with negligible resistance as prelude to a "100-hour ground war" (February 23 through 27) that ended in the inferno of a "highway of death" for routed Iraqi troops. This was, as the title of an official US Army history phrased it, a "whirlwind war."[1]

The second, related cause for jubilation came from seeing the "revolution in military affairs" in real time—and seeing this simultaneously as a decisive confirmation of America's unequivocal martial supremacy. This was a transitional moment, as military commentators put it, when the "industrial warfare" and relatively unguided ("dumb") explosives that characterized modern warfare since World War II were significantly, and spectacularly, enhanced by marvels such as stealth invisibility for aircraft and precision-guided ("smart") weapons.[2]

Although still a transformation in progress, the new world of warfare was highly visible. It was, indeed, exceptionally telegenic, with live round-the-clock media coverage almost turning the mayhem into the equivalent of a video game or Hollywood spectacle or play-by-play sporting event. (Some television footage even showed targets through the crosshairs of an American bomber's high-tech targeting system.) Outer space and cyberspace had become as critical as the traditional land-sea-air military domains. Satellites, lasers, and microcomputers steered precision-guided munitions (PGMs) including laser-guided bombs (LGBs) to their targets. Stealth fighter bombers evaded Iraqi radar. Infrared night-vision technology dispelled darkness. The Global Positioning System (GPS) made a significant contribution to what military jargon referred to as the "battlespace" and the "digitized battlefield." In popular parlance, the Gulf War was often referred to as "the computer war."[3]

A later think tank report on "the revolution in war" analyzed this technological transformation as consisting of major advances in ten "core military capabilities": awareness, connectivity, range, endurance, precision, miniaturization, speed, stealth, automation, and simulation. The phenomenal advances in "precision warfare" made possible by the digital revolution did not alter the Pentagon's abiding faith in the necessity of maintaining and exercising overwhelming military might in the form of airpower and other instruments of brute force. They simply added an addictive new level of sophistication to the bedrock postwar mission of maintaining "asymmetrical technological advantages" over the enemy.[4]

The concept and harsh complexities of "asymmetry" would come back to haunt America's warfighters a decade and more later, when nonstate terrorists and un-uniformed insurgents relying on rudimentary weapons and irregular warfare successfully challenged the ultra-sophisticated US military machine. Until then, however—and even thereafter—the never-ending quest to ensure asymmetrical technological superiority mesmerized the war planners.

In actual practice, the revolution in military affairs was not as transformative as its most fervent apostles declared. Although "smart bombs" and "surgical strikes" garnered headlines, precision-guided munitions only constituted some 7 to 8 percent of the munitions deployed in the Gulf War. (17,000 PGMs were expended, as opposed to 210,000 unguided bombs.) Victory still rested on the traditional American way of war: reliance on massive air and land power. The arsenal of "dumb" weapons included contro-versial explosives like cluster bombs (which spread large numbers of "bomblets" over areas as great as ten or more acres, and became notorious in the Vietnam War), "daisy cutters" (15,000-pound bombs also notorious from use in Vietnam, capable of destroying everything within a 600-yard radius), and armor-piercing deplet-ed-uranium munitions.

Aerial and missile attacks pulverized Iraqi military and civil-ian infrastructure for more than a month before land forces were committed to battle. There were more than 116,000 sorties by fixed-wing aircraft plus helicopters, about 85 percent of them by American crews. Total coalition losses were 63 US and 12 Allied aircraft—with only 42 of these losses occurring in combat and the rest in accidents. The volume of explosives delivered (88,500 tons) was roughly half the tonnage of bombs dropped on Japan in 1945, and the destruction of civilian or dual-use infrastructure, especially in Baghdad, was severe. Once airpower had done its job, the ground forces—featuring a variety of "new generation" tanks, helicopters, and the like—proceeded to deliver the coup de grâce to Iraqi land forces in the devastating "100-hour" battle that brought the conflict to a close.[5]

A few years after the war, a French diplomat used the pages of the American journal *Foreign Affairs* to call attention to the difficulty ordinary Iraqis had comprehending "the Allied ratio-nale for using airpower to systematically destroy or cripple Iraqi infrastructure and industry: electric power stations (92 percent of installed capacity destroyed), refineries (80 percent of production capacity), petrochemical complexes, telecommunications centers (including 135 telephone networks), bridges (more than 100), roads, highways, railroads, hundreds of locomotives and boxcars full of goods, radio and television broadcasting stations, cement plants, and factories producing aluminum, textiles, electric cables, and medical supplies."

As one example of the suffering this caused, he noted that "the paralysis of electric power plants deprived Iraqis of drinking water, interrupted agricultural irrigation through pumping stations, and clogged the sewage system. Garbage and debris accumulated, rats proliferated, and epidemics spread. Hospitals without generators were unable to perform surgery."[6]

Similar criticism was leveled by others, especially on the political left, and the official US rejoinder was twofold. It was argued that Iraq was able to recover from such destruction quickly. More telling, it was emphasized that the coalition's offensive had taken great care to avoid "collateral damage" involving civilians and noncombatants. An air force summary report actually identified "the trend toward 'bloodlessness' as a desideratum in the conduct of war."[7]

"Bloodlessness" amounted to plausible hyperbole of a sort that had become fashionable in military planning circles and "public diplomacy." It reflected a fundamental change from the saturation bombing of populated areas that characterized air war in World War II and in America's wars in Korea and Vietnam. On the coalition side, the label is indeed close to apt, and strong ammunition for the decline-in-violence argument. The tally for Gulf War fatalities is 148 US military personnel killed in action, including thirty-five by "friendly fire," plus around 150 deaths in noncombat accidents such as exploding munitions. Coalition fatalities, not including Kuwait, which Iraq had invaded, totaled less than one hundred.[8]

On the Iraqi side, estimates vary but are generally not especially high compared to major wars of the past. At one point, the Iraqi government itself put direct civilian fatalities in the air war at a low and implausibly precise 2,278 individuals. Most battle death estimates range from 20,000 to 35,000. Here, however, we again confront the question of war's lethal impact as reflected in broader and longer-term fatalities. Thus, a study by an American demographer published in 1993 concluded that the total Iraqi death count may have been close to 205,000 (56,000 soldiers and 3,500 civilians killed in battle; 35,000 killed in immediate postwar Kurdish and Shiite uprisings that the US government encouraged when the war ended, but failed to support; and 111,000 deaths attributable to "postwar adverse health effects" due to damage to the electrical grid, sewage and water-purification systems, health-care facilities, and domestic roads and distribution systems. By this calculation, approximately 70,000 of those who died from war-related health effects were children under fifteen and 8,500 were people over sixty-five.[9]

The seemingly decisive Gulf War victory produced not just euphoria among most Americans but also a sense of historical cleansing. A US Army booklet published two decades later, for example, still opened with the declaration that "the overwhelming success" in the Gulf War "renewed the confidence and assertiveness of the United States in its foreign policy in the Near East and throughout the world." The historical context for this renewal was explicit: "The Army at the end of the Cold War was a very different institution than the one that had emerged from the sting of defeat in Vietnam less than two decades before."[10]

This echoed President Reagan's bravado about standing tall after the invasion of Grenada, but that shaky boast was now reaffirmed by a triumph involving massed forces and massive might. President George H. W. Bush, Reagan's successor, repeated the goodbye-to-Vietnam mantra in the opening days of March 1991, following the rout of the Iraqi army. His words were delivered in two separate talks that are usually conflated. "By God," the president told a small audience in Washington on March 1, "we've kicked the Vietnam syndrome once and for all." The following day, in a radio address to armed forces in the Persian Gulf, he famously declared, "The specter of Vietnam has been buried forever in the desert sands of the Arabian Peninsula."[11]

Coinciding as it did with the demise of the Soviet Union, this martial ebullience reinforced confidence that the United States was now—fifty years after Henry Luce's vision of an American Century—truly in command. President Bush began broadcasting this vision even before Saddam Hussein's forces were crushed. On September 11, 1990, four months before Operation Desert Storm was launched, he described the buildup for war to Congress as an opportunity for the United States to lead the way toward "a new world order . . . freer from the threat of terror, stronger in the pursuit of justice, and more secure in the quest for peace." He reiterated this optimistic forecast on January 16, 1991, when announcing the first coalition air strikes against Iraq. In his State of the Union address on January 29, the president again envisioned a new world order in which "peace and security, freedom, and the rule of law" prevailed.[12]

Over the course of the 1990s, America's "new world order" paradigm was put into practice through several overlapping military initiatives. All had pre-1990 precedents, but double victory in the Cold War and Gulf War lifted them to new levels. One was an intense effort by all branches of the military to build on the lessons of the Gulf War in order to realize the full technological and organizational potential of the revolution in military affairs. A second realm of activity focused on redefining America's global mission in a post–Cold War world, with emphasis on regional trouble spots like the Middle East. This entailed strengthening paramilitary special operations forces and expanding an already sprawling global network of bases, while accelerating overt and covert "interventions" abroad.

At the same time, the 1990s saw a drastic revision of the doctrine of nuclear deterrence. In part, this involved significant reductions in the US and former Soviet (now Russian) nuclear arsenals. In part, it entailed redefining whom and what the surviving US arsenal was deterring. Eventually, this nuclear strategizing turned into a campaign to "modernize" existing stockpiles—a policy guaranteed, as the old nuclear arms race should have made clear, to spark a counter-response by other members of the proliferating "nuclear club."

The technological fixations, strategic formulations, and operational initiatives of Pentagon planners during this relatively optimistic decade were intense and elaborate. Where the revolution in military affairs was concerned, this produced a minefield of jargon and an alphabet soup of acronyms. This lexical effusion was accelerated by the fact that in practice computer networks in the "computer war" of 1991 actually had performed poorly when it came to ensuring battlefield cohesion and "interoperability." As a popular military metaphor put it, the services still remained "stovepiped"— locked into their own digital platforms and networks.

To rectify such compartmentalization, a great deal of theoretical and practical expertise was devoted to refining "network-centric warfare" and realizing an overarching "system of systems architecture." "C4I/SR" became a cherished acronym—referring to developing an integrated capacity in "command, control, communications, computers, intelligence" plus surveillance and reconnaissance. "High-altitude satellite architecture" (HASA) was integral to ensuring interoperability on the digital battlefield. So were "space-based infrared systems" (SBIRS) and "unmanned aerial vehicles" (UAV), known more popularly as drones.[13]

All service branches dedicated themselves to formulating and implementing "C4I for the Warrior" and "C4I for the 21st Century," catchphrases popularized in the early 1990s. The navy and marines, for example, did this under the project name "Copernicus." The army's counterpart initiative was called "Enterprise," and the air force's, "Horizon." No slogan was more resonant, however, than "full spectrum dominance," which was highlighted in two frequently cited mission statements by the Joint Chiefs of Staff: a July 1996 publication titled *Joint Vision 2010* and a May 2000 update titled *Joint Vision 2020*.

The 1996 JCS text proclaimed, "Full Spectrum Dominance will be the key characteristic we seek for our Armed Forces in the 21st century." *Joint Vision 2020* provided this succinct definition: "The label full spectrum dominance implies that U.S. forces are able to conduct prompt, sustained, and synchronized operations with combinations of forces tailored to specific situations and with access to and freedom to operate in all domains—space, sea, land, air, and information."[14]

In 1996, a university-based systems analyst conveyed the high expectations for the digitized battlespace in these words: "In the past, the key to successful warfighting was the best use of weapons. . . . In the future, the key to successful joint operations often will be the best use of information." Writing at the same time, a high-ranking navy strategist succinctly captured the fears as well as hopes that underlay US military thinking in the new world order. "The system-of-systems and RMA [revolution in military affairs],"

he wrote, "holds out the promise that in the not too distant future the pointed end of the spear may be smaller, far sharper and able to pierce the opponents [sic] jugular vein on the first throw." He then proceeded to ruminate about the fog of war in the "increasingly ambiguous and dangerous world" that had materialized since the Soviet Union disappeared as a "peer competitor"—a world in which "coalitions will parallel and perhaps replace alliances."[15]

This admixture of optimism and anxiety was, in fact, widespread in the 1990s. While public diplomacy offered paeans to a new world order of peace and security, mid-level Pentagon planners—backed by a small chorus of public intellectuals—were calling attention to a dystopian world of disorder. To these strategists and geopoliticians, the end of Cold War bipolarity and clear-cut ideological confrontation had brought not peace and security, but rather a world teetering on the verge of chaos, even near-anarchy.

In the public sphere, this was conveyed in catchphrases like Samuel Huntington's "clash of civilizations" (1993), Robert Kaplan's "the coming anarchy" (1994), and Ralph Peters's "new warrior class" (1994)—all depicting, in one way or another, the collapse of central governments and rise of religious, ethnic, and tribal violence, including terrorism, especially in the third world in general and Middle East in particular.

Writings by insider military analysts after the Cold War ended were similarly riddled with fear and foreboding: "global disintegration," "combustive vacuum," "Low Intensity Conflict" (LIC), "Grey Area Phenomena" (GAP), "Military Operations Other Than War" (MOOTW), and so on. An army training pamphlet titled *Force XXI Operations*, issued in 1994, presented various categories of potential twenty-first-century threats, including from "non-nation" entities—which, in turn, were rather esoterically subdivided into "subnational, anational, and metanational" categories. An influential mid-1990s assessment by Major General Mike Myatt of the marine corps, titled "Chaos in the Littorals," envisioned a "potentially catastrophic" world of natural disasters, failed states, chaotic population flows, humanitarian crises, and "the possibility of nuclear, biological, chemical, or environmental disasters on an as yet unheard of scale."[16]

In practice, old-style interventions continued apace alongside new tip-of-the-spear technologies. By one academic calculation, the United States engaged in 263 military operations, large and small, in the four-and-a-half decades between World War II and 2002, of which only one-third took place before 1991. The remaining 176 actions—often in conjunction with the United Nations and/or NATO, and usually undertaken in the name of preserving peace—occurred in the twelve years between 1991 and 2002. Some of these interventions were dramatic and more than a few failed to leave a residue of goodwill toward the United States or its partners.[17] As pointed out by critical scholars like Andrew Bacevich, a West Point graduate and Vietnam veteran, between 1980 and the terrorist attacks of September 11, 2001, US forces "invaded or occupied or bombed" a dozen countries in the Islamic world (Iran, Libya, Lebanon, Iraq, Kuwait, Somalia, Bosnia, Saudi Arabia, Afghanistan, Sudan, Kosovo, and Yemen).[18]

The corollary to these overseas operations was a global network of military installations that the political scientist Chalmers Johnson, a former consultant to the CIA, famously identified in 2004 as "America's empire of bases." Much of this empire reflected the Cold War legacy of "forward" bases established in Europe and Asia after World War II and the Korean War to "contain" communism, many of which were retained after the dissolution of the Soviet Union.

A good part of this military-base empire, on the other hand, reflected preoccupation with the Middle East in general and its oil in particular. This traced back to the Carter and Reagan doctrines of the 1980s, and was reinforced by the global-disintegration thinking of the 1990s. Collecting data on the eve of the second US invasion of Iraq in early 2003, Johnson calculated that the Pentagon's own bookkeeping indicated that the military "currently owns or rents 702 overseas bases" around the world. This was, in his view, an undercount. Johnson argued that in "an honest estimate, the actual size of our military empire would probably top 1,000 different bases in other people's countries." No one, he concluded, not even the Pentagon, actually knew precisely how many overseas facilities the United States maintained.[19]

Expansion of overseas bases was paralleled by a shift in operational focus by the US Navy—which, in its distinctive way, provided an armada of floating bases. In a white paper issued in 1992 that prefigured General Myatt's dramatic chaos-in-the-littorals formulation, this shift was defined as moving "from a focus on a global threat to a focus on regional challenges and opportunities." More precisely, this meant concentrating "on capabilities required in the complex operating environment of the 'littoral' or coastlines of the earth." "Dominance of littoral areas," this strategy statement went on, "means bombs, missiles, shells, bullets, and bayonets," including "deep" intervention by the marines where necessary.

Strategic writings in this vein repeatedly emphasize the necessity of denying "A2/AD" (area-access/area-denial) capabilities to adversaries or potential enemies that would challenge US domination not just of global offshore waters but of broad coastal land areas as well (extending scores or even hundreds of miles inland). It is not difficult to imagine how potential adversaries like China might have viewed such an aggressive redefinition of the American strategic mission, but there is little indication this was given serious consideration in the Pentagon. This shift from "blue water" operations to power projection in littoral areas became a naval mantra in the 1990s. A 1994 navy publication, for example, noted that "a U.S. warship is sovereign U.S. territory," no matter where it might be. In 1997, an updated statement clarified the high-tech dimension of the shift to a littoral focus: "We will take advantage of our robust command and control systems and the reach of our sensors and weapons to concentrate combat power from dispersed, networked forces and project power far inland." The objective of such forward deployment was to cripple enemy defenses, hit enemy offenses hard, and "achieve a quick *fait accompli*."[20]

US warships in offshore waters were not, of course, self-sufficient floating bases. They also required on-land facilities, thus helping explain the growth of the empire of bases that took off in the 1990s. The difficulty of quantifying this empire resembles the difficulty of quantifying and evaluating the scale, scope, nature, and human consequences of "war" and "conflict" since World War II. Precision is impossible. Still, the big picture of the speed and density with which America garrisoned the globe after the Cold War ended is clear, and it helps illuminate the rising tide of Islamist hatred of the United States that lay behind the September 11 atrocities.

Take, for example, the case of Saudi Arabia, which became the major staging area for the US and coalition forces that began mobilizing for the Gulf War in August 1990. Coalition aircraft operated out of some fifteen bases in Saudi Arabia during the war, and from 1992 to 2003 that kingdom continued to play a major role as a launching pad for US-led coalition aircraft enforcing a "no-fly zone" over southern Iraq. The physical presence of foreign troops on Saudi soil was especially offensive to many Muslims, who saw this as both desecration of the site of Islam's holiest places (Mecca and Medina) and symbolic of the country's subservience to America. Osama bin Laden, who masterminded the September 11 attacks, had publicly and passionately denounced the sacrilege of American boots on the soil of his native land as early as 1996.[21]

◆

What emerges here, as the twentieth century drew to a close, is an explosive overlay of developments. Fixation on Middle East oil, apocalyptic visions of chaos in the littorals, expansion of overseas military bases, acceleration of military interventions, the wishful thinking involved in assuming that monopolization of sophisticated military might ensures full-spectrum dominance or a quick fait accompli—all were drawing the United States ever deeper into a turbulent region that, on its own, had long been plagued with strife.

Major conflicts in the Greater Middle East in the decades since World War II included four wars between Pakistan and India (1947, 1965, 1971, 1999), relentless hostility and open clashes between Israel and nearby Arab and Muslim nations as well as stateless Palestinians (including wars in 1948–49, 1956, 1967–70, 1973, and 1982), the Algerian war of independence (1954–62), civil war in North Yemen (1962–70) and Lebanon (1975–90), the Iran-Iraq War (1980–88), endemic conflict between Turkey and the Kurds (especially intense from 1984 on), and a post-Soviet Afghanistan still ravaged by internal conflict.

Underlying these headline-garnering conflicts ran deep undercurrents of tribal, ethnic, and religious identity and animosity.

Pentagon planners agonized about this turbulence, but top-level policymakers, as it turned out, did not take it particularly seriously. All this set the stage for a new epoch of violence after September 11 and America's declaration of a "global war on terror."

CHAPTER 7

SEPTEMBER 11 AND "A NEW KIND OF WAR"

For the United States, the great wars of the twentieth century were all foreign wars. After repelling British forces in 1812–1815, the nation was blessed with territorial security. And after their brutal mid-nineteenth-century Civil War, Americans never again experienced the trauma of battle or bombardment on their own soil, apart from Japan's surprise attack on military targets in Hawaii on December 7, 1941, and the short "forgotten battle" to retake the remote US-owned Aleutian Islands from Japanese forces in 1943.

Servicemen who died in foreign wars were not forgotten: US veterans of World War I, World War II, the Korean War, and the Vietnam War continued to be memorialized. Commemorations of World War II and the Vietnam War in particular became occasions for reinforcing a carefully cultivated national sense of victimization and sacrifice. Still, this long history of physical isolation from intimate contact with war's horrors goes far toward helping explain the near-pathological shock that followed al-

Qaeda's attacks on the World Trade Center in New York and Pentagon in Washington on September 11, 2001.

The general US response to those attacks—carried out in hijacked planes by nineteen Islamist terrorists, fifteen of them Saudis—immediately prompted invocation of World War II. The assault was likened to both Japan's attack on Pearl Harbor and the suicidal Japanese kamikaze pilots who made an appearance in the closing stages of the Pacific War. Political pundits, especially conservatives, debated whether America was fighting "World War III" or "World War IV" (with the Cold War in the latter case being identified as World War III).

This was not marginal rhetoric as it turned out, for the George W. Bush administration—which included Vice President Dick Cheney and Secretary of Defense Donald Rumsfeld, both former Gulf War policymakers and strong promoters of the revolution in military affairs—turned such hysteria into concrete war policy. The United States, it was declared, was now embroiled in a "global war on terror," sometimes awkwardly identified as GWOT.

On September 15, four days after al-Qaeda's attack, the CIA produced a top-secret proposal titled "Worldwide Attack Matrix" that called for an antiterror campaign in eighty countries. Despite the classified nature of this recommendation, top officials lost no time conveying its general intent to the public. Rumsfeld, for instance, told reporters that the United States was looking at "a large multi-headed effort that probably spans 60 countries, including the United States." In a widely quoted television appearance, Cheney stated that the United States would have to work "sort of the dark side, if you will." Details of what these dark-side covert activities would involve (including torture) would not come to light until several years later, but the open reaction to the September 11 outrage came quickly. US forces, with especially strong

British support, launched war against the Taliban government in Afghanistan on October 7 and began preparing to invade Iraq. Seventeen months later, on March 19, 2003, they did so. Neither country had been responsible for the September 11 attacks.[1]

This swift, sweeping, militarized response reflected hubris as well as paranoia at the top levels of government. What changed the world, it has been perceptively observed, was not al-Qaeda's attack but Washington's overreaction.[2] "Global war" rhetoric carried with it visions of total and unconditional victory over a clearly defined enemy, as in World War II, a conflict American policymakers evoked frequently in the years following September 11 and the subsequent invasion of Iraq.[3] Declaration of war also reflected the overconfidence in US monopolization of cutting-edge military violence that was generated by the Gulf War. Invading Iraq, one of Rumsfeld's outside advisers on defense policy trumpeted publicly not once but twice, would be a "cakewalk." This was widely quoted.[4]

That the CIA was able to produce a "worldwide attack matrix" covering eighty countries almost overnight may seem impressive at first glance, at least to outsiders. In fact, it was not at all surprising. The military and intelligence community had been deeply engaged in similar global interventions—including Cheney's "dark side" practices—ever since World War II.

A few weeks after September 11, Rumsfeld published an op-ed essay titled "A New Kind of War." Later, in November 2002, during the buildup for invading Iraq, he told a radio call-in show that warnings of a quagmire were misplaced. "The idea that it's going to be a long, long battle of some kind I think is belied by the fact of what happened in 1990 [sic]," he said, referring to the Gulf War.

"Five days or five weeks or five months, but it certainly isn't going to last any longer than that."[5]

Rumsfeld's forecast was wildly inaccurate. Combat operations in Iraq continued until August 2010, and the last US troops were not withdrawn until the closing weeks of 2011—only to return three years later. By that time, terrorism and insurgency had metastasized throughout the Greater Middle East and northern Africa. By the middle of the second decade of the twenty-first century, as the two-term presidency of Barack Obama neared its end, the region was aflame and the United States was embroiled in military operations in Syria, Pakistan, Libya, Somalia, and Yemen, as well as Afghanistan (still) and Iraq (again). Al-Qaeda had been superseded in influence by a host of copycat terrorist organizations. ISIL (Islamic State of Iraq and the Levant)—also known as ISIS (Islamic State of Iraq and Syria) or simply IS (Islamic State)—had established a "caliphate" encompassing major parts of Iraq and Syria, and proclaimed authority over Muslims worldwide. While most terrorist atrocities involved Muslims killing Muslims, attacks had accelerated in Europe and the United States.

The title of Rumsfeld's op-ed essay, on the other hand, was unwittingly prescient. The war on terror—and subsequently on grassroots uprisings and insurgencies triggered or abetted by the US-led invasions—turned out to be a new kind of war indeed, albeit in ways almost antithetical to the high-tech, smart-weapon, rapid-deployment, small-footprint, in-and-out war he and a legion of erstwhile defense experts in Washington had envisioned. "Asymmetry" did indeed become the watchword of twenty-first-century conflict, but the almost religious faith in victory through "technological asymmetry" and "full spectrum dominance" was turned on its head. The Gulf War proving ground for the revolution in military affairs turned out to be less a harbinger of future warfare than a mirage of irresistible American power.[6] Unlike conventional conflicts, including the Gulf War, the new kind of war did not involve a clash of uniformed forces representing sovereign states and engaging one another in relatively fixed formations. The new antagonists were nonstate actors who had neither a formal military structure nor fixed geographical identity. While American policymakers tried to argue that some sort of state support lay behind the September 11 attacks—thus rationalizing the invasions of Afghanistan and Iraq—their immediate response was an acknowledgement of the elusive transnational nature of terrorism. The CIA's "worldwide attack matrix" reflected this reality of an amorphous, ubiquitous, place-shifting, shape-shifting, name-shifting enemy. What it did not reflect—despite a full decade of intense and often agonizing interservice strategizing about low-intensity conflict and chaos in the littorals—was any genuinely serious appreciation of the deep schisms and contradictions in Middle Eastern societies or any serious expectation that foreign invasion would ignite indigenous blowback extending to violent insurrection.

Both Afghanistan and Iraq provided opportunities for US forces to display their awesome firepower in the opening stages of their two invasions. In Afghanistan, along with precision-guided bombs and missiles, this included several 15,000-pound daisy-cutters (dropped on caves in which Osama bin Laden was thought to be hiding) and more than 1,200 cluster munitions that scattered several hundred thousand bomblets. The invasion of Iraq opened similarly with media-pleasing "shock and awe" pyrotechnics that included some four-score cruise missiles fired at Baghdad (plus four satellite-guided 2,000-pound "bunker busters" that missed their targets). Two-thirds of the opening air campaign involved precision-guided "smart" munitions (as opposed to less than 8 percent in the Gulf War), and their contribution to the quick downfall of Saddam Hussein was decisive.

Almost as quickly, however, it became clear that once Iraq's overwhelmed conventional forces had been dispatched, high-tech weaponry was of limited use against lightly armed "pop-up" moving targets. The terrorist (and, later, insurrectionary) foes were far from being Luddites. They made effective use of cell phones, laptop computers, the Internet, and social media. Their more sophisticated theorists even produced tracts that call to mind the CIA and School of the Americas manuals of the 1960s through 1980s, which similarly used academic scaffolding to reinforce tutelage in terror. An even closer analogy is to be found in the case-study textbooks churned out by Western business schools. A text whose title translates as *The Management of Savagery: The Most Critical Stage through which the Umma [Islamic State] Will Pass* became the epitome of this. Published on the Internet in 2004, this tome (268 pages in translation) makes extensive reference to American and European management studies.[7]

Such up-to-date touches in the terrorist camp meshed with a shrewd grasp of popular psychology. This extended not just to exploiting the resentments of potential recruits but also to an uncanny ability to bait and unnerve distant and ostensibly far more powerful and "rational" enemies. At the same time, the weapons of the terrorists generally remained primitive: Kalashnikov AK-47 assault rifles, machine guns, rocket-propelled grenades, mortars, devastatingly effective improvised explosive devices (IEDs), and of course suicide bombers. Fighters crisscrossed the battle-space in pickup trucks, relying on extreme brutality and waves of grassroots insurgency provoked, in large part, by the foreign invasions. These low-intensity tactics proved significantly more effective—and more rational, given the setting—than America's carefully networked maneuvers and gold-plated arsenals.

This new kind of irregular conflict—pitting governments and their allies against opponents motivated less by ideology than by religious fervor, sectarian differences, tribal and ethnic rivalries, and plain misery—forced the planners who rested faith in technological asymmetry to rethink their premises. Encountering near-anarchy firsthand brought this, painfully, out of the realm of 1990s-style armchair theorizing. There were no jugular-piercing spear points or quick faits accomplis. There was, on the other hand, intense blowback as death and dislocation mounted among the ordinary people of Iraq and Afghanistan. As one chastened American analyst eventually put it, "The real revolution in military affairs is forcing modern states to use the advancement in military technology to focus on minimizing civilian casualties and collateral damage rather than destroying the enemy."[8]

In a way, terror and psychological warfare were flipped in this new kind of war. Terror tactics are as old as warfare, and state terror runs a close second in historical precedents. Terror bombing, on the other hand, has a certain modern and contemporary ring. From World War II through the Korean and Vietnam Wars, this was associated primarily with air attacks on urban centers and noncombatant populations aimed at destroying enemy morale. In Vietnam, however, all-out air war was already proving counterproductive. The enemy did not break psychologically, while media depictions back home of these terrifying attacks contributed to erosion of American popular support for the war. (Contrary to the "Vietnam syndrome" thesis, this revulsion had little to do with adroit North Vietnamese propaganda and a great deal to do with television coverage of a shocking intimacy absent in World War II and Korea.) Military planners welcomed the relatively "bloodless" nature of smart weapons in the Gulf War not just because this kept American casualties down but also because it promised to all but eliminate the stigma of deliberately targeting noncombatants.

In the new era of post–September 11 warfare, it was the terror tactics of al-Qaeda and its successors that assumed center stage. These atrocities differed in nature and scale from mechanistically killing civilians at a distance. Their perpetrators flaunted them as a signature statement. The physical proximity and suicidal relationship between the bomber and his or her victims compounded the horror in the public eye, as it was meant to do. There was, in these more intimate acts of murder, a macabre element of theater.

The character, manipulation, and destabilizing effectiveness of such terrorism differed in numerous ways from the state terror long practiced by large and small nations. In the digital world of instantaneous mass communication and sensationalism, this, too, was a new kind of war. Religious fanaticism compounded the horror of this latest incarnation of callous terror. The bedrock objective of breaking the morale of perceived enemies, however, was old.

As the entanglements in Afghanistan and Iraq dragged on, it became clear that this was also a new kind of war when it came to bureaucratic sprawl and organizational contradictions. On the one hand, computer-focused theories like network-centric warfare presented an idealized vision of streamlined command-and-control operations. At the same time, however, the extreme response to September 11 gave birth in the United States to a public and private "security" complex more gargantuan, cumbersome, compartmentalized, faction-ridden, redundant, wasteful, corrupt, and nontransparent than anything the nation had seen before. Top-echelon military and civilian intelligence agencies proliferated (there were seventeen by 2014), and this was only the tip of the iceberg. There were no body counts here, only immeasurable violence done to civil society in general. A striking feature of this new Leviathan was the extent to which activities traditionally handled by the government or military were outsourced. Many underlying dynamics drove this wholesale privatization. These included budgetary pressures affecting defense spending, especially after the Gulf War, coupled with military and political calculations that outsourcing would help disguise real spending and at the same time appeal to popular sentiment favoring a smaller military "footprint." Political chicanery and budgetary skullduggery played a role in these developments, but of greater impact were neoliberal as well as neoconservative arguments in favor of deregulation, privatization, and market fundamentalism of the sort championed by Ronald Reagan and England's prime minister Margaret Thatcher. Still, it took September 11 and the panic over domestic as well as overseas "security" to jolt privatization to a drastically new level militarily. The inevitable obverse side of this hysteria was accelerated militarization of the private sector. Fear of terror proved lucrative.

By 2007, for example, around 60 percent of the CIA's workforce consisted of private contractors. In 2010, a two-year journalistic investigation of "Top Secret America" by the *Washington Post* found that "some 1,271 government organizations and 1,931 private companies work on programs related to counterterrorism, homeland security and intelligence in about 10,000 locations across the United States." Two-thirds of these programs operated under the Department of Defense. By that date, an estimated 854,000 military officials, civil servants, and private contractors held top-secret security clearances.[9]

Such massive outsourcing was replicated in the battlespace itself. In the decade-plus following September 11, the number of nonmilitary personnel supported by the United States in Afghanistan and Iraq was commonly equivalent to or greater than the number of US troops deployed. At the peak of these military occupations (between 2007 and 2010), this meant funding upwards of a quarter-million contract workers in the two countries alongside a comparable number of troops. Most of this civilian labor fell under the Defense Department budget, but major reliance on outsourcing extended to the State Department, Agency for International Development, and Department of Homeland Security.

Civilians always have provided support for military operations, but the scale of private services in the war on terror was unprecedented. This becomes clear when outsourcing after September 11 is set against the civilian-to-military personnel ratio in prior US conflicts. In World War I, the estimated ratio was 1:24; in World War II, 1:7; in the Vietnam War, 1:5; in the short Gulf War a remarkable 1:104; in Iraq in 2007, 1:0.8; in Afghanistan in 2009, 1:0.7; and in Iraq in 2010, 1:1.[10]

Large numbers of contractors profited from these arrangements, and two caveats are commonly offered concerning the services they provided. First, the bulk of civilians employed were engaged in noncombat tasks such as preparing meals, cleaning, doing laundry, providing transportation and storage facilities, laboring in construction projects, or serving as language specialists. Second, the recruitment of workers, especially at the more unskilled levels, tapped both local nationals and an international pool of cheap third world labor—upwards of thirty different nationalities in the case of Iraq. At the same time, however, private contractors also provided more specialized and remunerative services ranging from major construction projects and paramilitary and mercenary tasks to maintaining some of the complex systems associated with the revolution in military affairs.[11]

Much outsourcing was inefficient and corrupt, and a small but significant portion was criminal. One such undertaking— "outsourcing torture" under a program euphemistically called "extraordinary rendition"—was statistically miniscule but morally appalling. Orchestrated by the CIA, this involved abducting foreign terrorist suspects and transferring them for secret detention and interrogation to the prisons of more than fifty nations around the world. It was, in a grotesque way, almost as if the cross-border renditions of Operation Condor during the dirty wars in Latin America three decades earlier had been resurrected on a global scale, now orchestrated out of Washington.[12]

The overconfidence in technological superiority that led planners to anticipate a short, sweet military campaign in the Middle East had a predictable financial corollary. Projected dollar costs for the war on terror, especially in Iraq, were grossly underestimated. Rumsfeld, for instance, put the price tag for overthrowing Saddam Hussein at around $50 billion. Other officials argued that oil revenues from Iraq itself would be sufficient to cover the costs of the US invasion and occupation. When the president's chief economic adviser broke ranks and told the *Wall Street Journal* that war costs might run as high as $100 to $200 billion, he was roundly criticized and soon relieved of his duties.[13]

Over a decade later, official tabulations of appropriations for the Afghan and Iraq wars put the direct costs from fiscal year 2001 to fiscal year 2015 at upwards of $1.6 trillion. Like the Pentagon's annual "base budget," however, this bookkeeping is misleading, for it excludes major long-term financial commitments including extensive medical-disability care for US veterans plus servicing the debt incurred to finance these wars. Thus, a highly regarded faculty research study published by Harvard's Kennedy School in 2013 concluded that "the Iraq and Afghanistan conflicts, taken together, will be the most expensive wars in US history—totaling somewhere between \$4 to \$6 trillion." Other independent studies also emphasize that the commonly cited government figures represent "only a fraction of the total war costs," and the United States will be paying for these undertakings over the next forty-plus years. The generally neglected projected costs—human as well as fiscal—are sobering. As of 2013, for instance, more than half of the 1.56 million US veterans of these wars who had left active service and thus qualified for medical care at Veterans Administration facilities had already applied for permanent disability benefits. Where the debt is concerned, some \$2 trillion was borrowed to finance the wars, amounting to 20 percent of the total \$9 trillion added to the national debt between 2001 and 2012.[14]

The Afghan and Iraq wars were also new—or relatively so—in that US battle deaths were conspicuously lower than in World War II, Korea, and Vietnam. This had been true of the short Gulf War, but unlike that "whirlwind" conflict the GWOT wars dragged on for years. As in all its foreign military engagements, the number of Americans killed was small compared to deaths on the other side. (The Department of Veterans Affairs puts US battle deaths in World War II at 291,557, plus "non-theater" service deaths at 113,842. The official total for battle deaths plus other "in theater" deaths in the Korean War is 36,574. For the Vietnam War, the counterpart Veterans Affairs total is 58,220.) Brown University's Watson Institute, whose "Costs of War" project collates input from close to forty researchers in different disciplines, calculates that from 2001 through 2014 US battle deaths in Afghanistan and Iraq totaled slightly more than 6,800. Roughly half were from roadside bombs (IEDs) and rocket-propelled grenade fire. These figures are noteworthy, but only a small part of the picture. They do not include disturbed veterans who died from drug overdoses, suicide, vehicle crashes, and the like after being discharged. More significantly, they do not address the scale of overall deaths among non-Americans. Here, the Costs of War project calculated that conflict in Afghanistan and Iraq (plus Pakistan) from 2001 through 2014 resulted in over 370,000 direct war deaths, including armed forces on all sides plus civilians, contractors, journalists, and humanitarian workers. Some 210,000 of these violent deaths were civilians. Many direct deaths came from insurrection and internecine religious and political strife triggered or unleashed by the US incursions. Indirect deaths from war-related causes such as malnutrition, damaged health systems, poor sanitation, and lack of clean water probably exceeded the "direct war deaths" number. Beyond this, at the end of 2015 the number of Afghan and Iraqi war refugees and internally displaced persons was over 6.5 million.[15]

Another critical assessment of the "body count" of the first ten years of the war on terror, published in 2015 by the Nobel Prize–winning Physicians for Social Responsibility and two collaborating international organizations, reached the even higher "conservative estimate" that this conflict had, "directly or indirectly, killed around 1 million people in Iraq, 220,000 in Afghanistan and 80,000 in Pakistan, i.e. a total of around 1.3 million." While this total "could also be in excess of 2 million," this hundred-page report concluded, "a figure below 1 million is extremely unlikely."[16]

To such mortality and population displacement estimates must be added war-related disabilities. Here again, the data for Americans is fairly copious but virtually nonexistent for most of the rest of the world. At the same time, the upfront official data for the US side can, as usual, be misleading. Department of Defense reports, for instance, put the number of troops "wounded in action" in the GWOT wars at around fifty thousand. By contrast, as of early 2015 studies attentive to war-related mental-health disorders calculated that at least 970,000 American veterans of these conflicts had received some degree of official recognition for physical or, more commonly, psychological injuries. Where mental disorders are concerned, diagnostic categories tend to be porous—that is, post-traumatic stress disorder (PTSD), traumatic brain injury (TBI), and depression overlap. Harm and trauma extend to family and loved ones. Much of what is known in the jargon as "invisible wounds" is suffered in silence and not reported.[17]

What is now identified as PTSD is itself new on the scene as a recognized mental disorder. Known by colloquial (and often pejorative) terms like "shell shock" or "battle fatigue" in earlier conflicts, PTSD was not even formally recognized until 1980—seven years after the US military withdrew from Vietnam—when the American Psychiatric Association added it to the revised third edition of its *Diagnostic and Statistical Manual of Mental Disorders*. The prevalence of blast injuries from exploding IEDs in Iraq drew increased attention to the physical as opposed to purely psychological nature of combat-related mental disorders. What is new is not the suffering, but the belated acknowledgment of how extensive it is, and how inadequately it has been addressed until recently. Also new, at the same time, is the degree to which the GWOT wars were accompanied by more generous health-care benefits for veterans, extending to mental and emotional disorders—all of which add greatly to the projected long-term costs of these wars.

Statistics pertinent to war-related mental disorders vary. Veterans Administration studies postulate that in the protracted post-9/11 wars in Afghanistan and Iraq, the number of PTSD cases among US personnel amounted to between 11 percent and 20 percent in any given year. Looking back to earlier wars, these studies conclude that 30 percent of Vietnam War veterans experienced PTSD at one time or another, with 15 percent still diagnosed with the symptoms in the late 1980s. For the Gulf War of 1991, so widely celebrated for being short and virtually free of casualties on the victors' side, the PTSD estimate is 12 percent.[18] The 2013 Kennedy School report on projected costs of the Iraq and Afghanistan wars refers to the situation among returning veterans as a long-term "mental health epidemic," and notes that "research from previous wars has shown that these veterans are at higher risk for lifelong medical problems, such as seizures, decline in neurocognitive functioning, dementia and chronic diseases."[19]

The psychological legacy of war to great numbers of those dispatched to fight becomes even clearer when these rather abstract percentages and pathologies are set against the number of Americans deployed to fight in the country's three most recent major wars: some 2.7 million to Vietnam, a half million or so to the Gulf War, and upwards of 2.7 million to Iraq and Afghanistan.[20]

Operationally, psychologically, and pathologically, the new kind of war also resonated with America's warfighting past. Take the reduction of the enemy and most of the world's problems to a single word. "Terror," for all practical purposes, replaced "communism" as the great evil. "In many ways," President Bush typically stated after the invasions of Afghanistan and Iraq, "this fight resembles the struggle against communism in the last century." It was, he declared on another occasion, a fight "between good and evil" in which there could be "no neutral ground." Much like the Cold

War, the new war became a holy war on all sides—although the Islamist fundamentalism of the terrorists sharpened the explicitly theological edge of this in ways not seen in prior modern wars.[21]

On the US side, postulation of a Manichaean world was not confined to propaganda for public consumption. It permeated decision-making circles after World War II, reaching a catastrophic apogee in the Vietnam War. Years afterwards, Robert McNamara, who served as secretary of defense from 1961 to 1968, offered a concise explanation for US failure in that conflict. In a filmed interview in 2003, when he was in his mid-eighties, McNamara spoke of the need to know one's enemies—to "empathize" with them, and "try to put ourselves inside their skin and look at us through their eyes, just to understand the thoughts that lie behind their decisions and their actions."

He and his fellow Vietnam War policymakers, McNamara confessed, had viewed that conflict through the prism of the Cold War and ignored Vietnam's long struggle against colonialism, as well as the civil war that had divided the country since World War II. There had been a profound ignorance of history, of schisms within global communism, and of the nature, motivations, and resilience of the Vietnamese enemy.[22]

McNamara's mea culpa was delivered at the very moment that the United States was embarking on its invasion of Iraq and dismissing, as Rumsfeld and his peers in Washington did so casually, any possibility of a quagmire. Despite warnings from middle-echelon military and civilian analysts, no one at top planning levels was capable of imagining that such a massive military intrusion could backfire and strengthen rather than diminish terrorism. No contingency planning to counter possible serious grassroots resistance, let alone insurgency, was included in the exuberant "shock and awe" playbook for the invasion. When the army and marine corps finally got around to publishing a new *Counterinsurgency* field manual, in December 2006, it opened with an acknowledgment that "counterinsurgency operations generally have been neglected in broader American military doctrine and national security policies since the end of the Vietnam War over 30 years ago."[23]

Given what we know of the 1980s and 1990s, this seems counterintuitive and almost inconceivable at first glance. Support for authoritarian regimes in Latin America by the School of the Americas, coupled with the Reagan administration's support of the Contras in Nicaragua, was all about abetting the suppression (or incitement) of dissent and insurgency. By much the same measure, the crushing defeat of the Soviet Union by lightly armed Afghan and foreign mujahedeen in Afghanistan a little more than a decade before September 11 amounted to a successful insurgency the United States itself helped fund and arm. The 1990s witnessed a flood of military studies and reports voicing alarm at the "increasingly ambiguous and dangerous" nature of the post–Cold War world, especially in the Middle East.

Despite this, the charge of neglect leveled in the 2006 counterinsurgency field manual is accurate. Much of the CIA's covert activity apparently did not influence mainstream strategizing. The insurgent victory in Afghanistan was largely dismissed as a revelation of Soviet ineptitude, and did not register in any meaningful way on the strategic radar of top planners and defense intellectuals. Most astonishing, after Vietnam the elite military academies that trained career officers actually expunged counterinsurgency from their regular curricula.[24]

In 2006, shortly before the new field manual was issued to great fanfare, retired general Jack Keane, a former vice chief of staff of the army who served in both Vietnam and Iraq, anticipated the handbook's prefatory confession of delinquency. "After the Vietnam War," he told a television audience, "we purged ourselves of everything that had to do with irregular warfare or insurgency, because it had to do with how we lost that war. In hindsight, that was a bad decision."[25]

This was more than just a bad decision. Beyond being a remarkable manifestation of groupthink, such willful narrow-mindedness reflected an inbred and abiding aversion to seeing either the world or oneself as seen by others, especially antagonists or potential antagonists. The Vietnam syndrome argument—that the United States lost the war in Vietnam because of a failure of will—was a red herring. Before as well as after the delusory whirlwind victory in the 1991 Gulf War, what was actually buried in the sand was common sense and any genuinely serious attempt at topmost levels to comprehend complex "inferior" enemies. McNamara was whistling in the wind when he spoke of this in 2003, as the United States was launching its hubristic invasion of Iraq. In this regard, the disastrous war on terror was not a new kind of war at all.

The price the world paid for such groupthink was a new world of instability.

CHAPTER 8

ARCS OF INSTABILITY

The most popular Cold War catchphrase conveying the distorted picture of monolithic communism that Robert McNamara later repudiated was the "domino theory." This traced back to the mid-1950s, when the United States replaced the military forces of colonial France in Vietnam. If indigenous communist forces fighting to unite that divided country succeeded, it was declared, this would set off a chain reaction throughout Asia in which country after country fell under Moscow-led communist domination, up to and including Japan.[1]

The worldwide proxy wars both Cold War superpowers had engaged in reflected the ubiquity of this sort of chain-reaction alarmism; and this mindset on the part of American strategic analysts did not disappear with the demise of the Soviet Union. It was redirected and reformulated in response to new perceived threats—a process already articulated in the Carter Doctrine of 1980, with its warning about the menace posed by the sudden emergence of the revolutionary Islamic Republic of Iran.

The domino metaphor did not survive the Cold War. In the 1990s, catchphrases of the chaos-in-the-littorals sort drew attention in US military circles, and by the turn of the century it had become common to speak of a world imperiled by an "arc of instability." A top-level intelligence report in 2004 captured the panoramic sweep of this, calling attention to "a great arc of instability from Sub-Saharan Africa, through North Africa, into the Middle East, the Balkans, the Caucasus and South and Central Asia and through parts of Southeast Asia."[2]

In this and other government reports, the arc of instability was associated with contradictions in the megatrend of globalization. On the one hand, globalization promised a world in which technological advances created a more integrated and prosperous international system. On the other hand, these high-tech, high-speed developments were exacerbating inequalities and heightening tensions between "haves" and "have-nots," both among and within nations. The disruptive side of globalization was the fertile ground in which protest and agitation, including radical Islamist-led terrorism, could take root. Even while propagating a strident gospel of antiglobalization coupled with anti-Westernization, such protest flourished by exploiting the new information technology to propagandize its cause while maintaining a decentralized mode of operation.[3]

The highly visible US wars, occupations, and interventions that followed September 11 were responses to this perception of ever-widening arcs of instability. Less visible were the extensive operations undertaken by covert US military units specializing in "unconventional warfare." When the Bush administration ended in January 2009, these elite special forces were deployed in around sixty nations. This was twenty countries less than the secret "worldwide attack matrix" the CIA produced following the

September 11 attacks but exactly what Rumsfeld had predicted publicly. A little over a year later, the press put the number of countries involved at seventy-five. In 2011, a spokesman for US Special Operations Command disclosed that, on any given day, American military personnel were indeed engaged in a range of missions in around seventy nations, but by year's end the total number of countries would be around 120. In 2014, a Department of Defense press release noted in passing that between 2011 and 2014 "special operations forces deployed into more than 150 countries." (As of 2011, the United Nations listed 193 recognized nations.) Like US operations conducted before the war on terror, the missions of these deployments ran the gamut from assassination and sabotage to intelligence and counterintelligence, from training and assisting foreign forces to engaging in humanitarian assistance.[4]

The Obama administration, under which special operations proliferated, also gave priority to a "surgical" counterterrorism undertaking that provoked great controversy: targeted assassinations by drones. Even the nomenclature of these operations was sinister. The two "remotely piloted aircraft" (RPA) involved were named Predator and Reaper; they carried Hellfire missiles; targets were selected at the White House from a "kill list."

Remote-controlled aircraft had been used in a few bombing missions in World War II, and for battlefield surveillance with still cameras in Vietnam. It was not until 1995, however, that drones were upgraded technologically and fitted with video cameras—and not until after September 11 that these reconnaissance vehicles were converted into precision-guided assassins. To their mostly American operators, the Predators and Reapers epitomized both the revolution in military affairs and a commitment to minimize US combat casualties and "collateral damage."[5]

The first weaponized Predator attacks were launched in Afghanistan in late 2001, as part of the air war against the Islamic fundamentalist Taliban movement that governed the country from 1996 to December 2001. The first targeted drone killing, directed by the CIA, took place in Afghanistan the following February. It was aimed at a "tall man" mistakenly identified as Osama bin Laden and killed three impoverished rural men instead. In 2002, drone strikes were directed against suspected terrorists in Yemen; in 2004, the CIA began targeting suspects in Pakistan; and in 2007, the assassination campaign was extended to Somalia.[6]

Estimates of the number of drone strikes and individuals killed vary but are not large. In April 2015, a reputable source calculated that 3,852 individuals had been killed in a total of 522 strikes. Of the dead, 476 were identified as "civilians." Contrary to what policymakers in Washington anticipated, however, the dramatic nature of these strikes gave them a concreteness and intimacy that highlighted the detached, dehumanized, mechanistic nature of precision-guided killing. Rather than enlist approbation for attempting to minimize collateral damage, the drone attacks became a symbol of secretive, irresponsible, no-risk terrorism on the part of the Americans. They were not only "an executioner's weapon," as one commentator observed, but also an ironic and exemplary "blowback weapon." They provoked anger, created gnawing fear among the populations over whom Predators and Reapers hovered, invited retaliation, and helped attract recruits to the terrorist cause.[7]

Military operations in roughly three-quarters of all the sovereign states in the world—coupled with high-tech assassinations even in nations with which the United States was not at war—suggest that the figurative arc of instability had been transformed into something else. But what? An ocean of instability? A shifting of geopolitical tectonic plates that threatened to destabilize every corner of the world?

By mid 2014, the *Wall Street Journal* was announcing that the United States confronted a "breadth of global instability" unseen "since the late 1970s . . . when the Soviet Union invaded Afghanistan, revolutionary Islamists took power in Iran, and Southeast Asia was reeling in the wake of the US exit from Vietnam."[8] Initially, the "arc of instability" formulation had downplayed any potential conflicts between major powers and focused primarily on parts of the Middle East, Africa, and Asia. Now the fear of Islamist terror, coupled with "failed nations" and disruptive "rogue states," was compounded by visions of great-power threats from an ascendant China, a reassertive Russia, and—until 2015—a near-nuclear Iran.

This heightened anxiety was further intensified by the resurrection in new guise of an old technological dread—nothing less than the specter of an "atomic arc of instability." Fifteen years after the collapse of the Soviet Union and end of the nuclear arms race, nuclear terror was back in the picture. This time, as articulated by American strategic thinkers beginning around 2005, it took the form of "a solid front of nuclear armed states" stretching over four thousand miles "from the Persian Gulf to the Sea of Japan, running through Iran, Pakistan, India, China and North Korea, with Russia looming from above." Nor did this ominous arc of nuclear (and nuclear-capable) states stand alone. There was the added terrifying possibility that nonstate terrorists might also acquire nuclear weapons.[9]

Predictably absent from most of these alarming prognostications was the fact that US nuclear policy itself was and remains a major provocation in the atomic arc of instability. One grave pitfall of obsessive immersion in self-centered "defense" thinking is that resultant policies are commonly, and not unreasonably, seen as threatening by others. The ceaseless US quest to maintain massive "technological asymmetry" militarily is guaranteed to keep arms races of every sort going.

◆

The collapse of the Soviet Union did not signal the demise of deterrence theory. Instead, what replaced Cold War deterrence doctrine in US strategic planning was a significantly revised projection of threats and targets. In the new nuclear paradigm, Russia was overshadowed by "rogue states" as well as China. (The term "rogue states" was popularized by top officials in the administration of President Bill Clinton in the mid-1990s and reincarnated as George W. Bush's notorious "axis of evil" targeting Iraq, Iran, and North Korea.) At the same time, "deterrence" and "counter-proliferation" were reinterpreted to include deterring chemical, biological, and radiological "weapons of mass destruction," and not just potential nuclear threats.[10]

This redefined mission provoked internal debate, but the upshot of the new paradigm was far-reaching. As the Pentagon's Defense Special Weapons Agency observed in 1997, the international environment had "evolved from a 'weapon rich environment' to a 'target rich environment.'" Nuclear weapons might be reduced in number, but their envisioned role was expanding. New emphasis was placed on "nonstrategic nuclear force employment" and limited or regional nuclear operations—meaning greater focus on improved tactical nuclear weapons involving less "collateral damage." This included, among other things, the development of "mini-nukes."[11]

A secret 1995 memorandum by planners in the US Strategic Command conveyed the revised outlook bluntly. "Since we believe it is impossible to 'uninvent' nuclear weapons or to prevent the clandestine manufacture of some number of them," the memo stated, these weapons were destined to remain the centerpiece of strategic deterrence. Their effectiveness would be enhanced, moreover, if the United States refrained from "negative security assurances" (such as no first use, or pledging never to use nuclear weapons against non-nuclear states). The challenge was "how best to induce terror in the mind of an adversary" to dissuade him from using any kind of weapon of mass destruction, whether nuclear or otherwise. To this end, the memo continued, it was desirable to create a climate of uncertainty and keep in mind that "it hurts to portray ourselves as too fully rational and cool-headed. . . . That the US may become irrational and vindictive if its vital interests are attacked should be part of the national persona we project to all adversaries."[12] Essentially, this amounted to Nixon's old madman theory redux. As usual, little consideration was given to the possibility that members of the burgeoning nuclear club might be persuaded to think and act similarly.

Maintaining nuclear deterrence and expanding its strategic applicability did not require maintaining stockpiles at Cold War levels. On the contrary, beginning in 1989—two years before the dissolution of the Soviet Union and its replacement by Russia, its diminished successor—the erstwhile superpower adversaries agreed to initiate drastic cuts in the strategic triad of long-range intercontinental ballistic missiles, submarine-launched ballistic missiles, and strategic bombers. The United States ceased production of new nuclear weapons in 1990, and in October 1992 the first President Bush signed into law a unilateral declaration to forego full-scale weapons testing.[13]

Estimates of the US and Soviet/Russian nuclear stockpiles vary, but the ballpark figures are clear enough. According to one detailed dataset, in 1991, when the Soviet Union dissolved, the

US nuclear stockpile stood at around 20,400 warheads and the Soviet stockpile around 34,600. In the critical triad of strategic warheads, the numbers were 9,300 for the United States (plus roughly 2,500 warheads based overseas, mostly in Europe) and 9,202 for the Soviet Union, which maintained over 23,000 nonstrategic warheads developed with the possibility of future conflict in Europe in mind. By 2001, the US strategic arsenal had been reduced to 6,196 warheads (plus 460 warheads still remaining overseas) and Russian strategic warheads to 5,263.[14]

September 11 and its chaotic aftermath brought to a head the tension between genuinely thoroughgoing nuclear disarmament and repurposing the nuclear deterrent for possible localized conflicts. On the one hand, the shock of the terrorist attacks convinced advocates of a flexible nuclear mission that it was now all the more urgent to retool the arsenal for potential use against multiple prospective threats. At the same time, however—and in a contrary direction—the specter of nuclear weapons falling into the hands of nonstate terrorists eventually persuaded many strategists to reverse course and argue that "deterrence theory" had become not merely irrelevant but dangerous. The urgent challenge, in this latter view, was to eliminate such deadly weapons entirely before they fell into the hands of suicidal adversaries who did not play by the old rules of the game.

George W. Bush's administration, which took office in January 2001, continued the process of incrementally reducing nuclear stockpiles in tandem with Russia. At the same time, it embraced the full-spectrum-dominance doctrine that became the Defense Department's "conceptual template" in the mid-1990s. That this spectrum incorporated the new nuclear paradigm percolating in Pentagon circles became clear in guidelines like the *Nuclear Posture Review* submitted to Congress at the end of 2001.

This review dismissed relying on an offensive nuclear force as the nation's sole deterrent strategy as "inappropriate for deterring the potential adversaries we will face in the 21st century." While Russia and, even more threatening, China were still targeted, the list of potential adversaries identified by name where the use of nuclear weapons was now considered possible included Iraq, North Korea, Iran, Syria, and Libya. Beyond this, other "well-recognized current dangers" that might entail nuclear deterrence or possible use included interstate conflict in the Middle East, or in divided Korea, or involving "the status of Taiwan."[15] (Always hovering in the background was apprehension of possible first use of nuclear weapons by Pakistan, India, or Israel.)

To meet this "diverse set of potential adversaries and unexpected threats" required not a capacity for massive retaliation, but rather a flexible "new mix" of nuclear, non-nuclear, and defensive capabilities. In planning documents, this mix was identified as a "global strike" capability involving "threatened (or actual) preemptive attacks on very-high value targets that will only be exposed for brief periods." Such a global-strike mix would "primarily rely upon long-range, high-speed, kinetic (advanced conventional and nuclear) and non-kinetic effects, unmanned systems, cyber systems, and/or small numbers of special operations forces employed over extended distances."[16]

The option of responding to perceived threats preemptively was not new. This had been implicit from early on in "first strike" nuclear theorizing. Mixing the nuclear deterrent with conventional weapons, and possibly responding with both to localized and non-nuclear threats, also had advocates from an early date (as William Perry's recollections emphasized) but was nonetheless a significant departure insofar as high-level planning was concerned. It turned nuclear warheads into potential warfighting weapons and so directed attention to production of low-yield warheads that theoretically could be used in tactical operations. It also placed a premium on creating—as the *Nuclear Posture Review* put it—"a revitalized nuclear weapons complex" that would "be able, if directed, to design, develop, manufacture, and certify new warheads in response to new national requirements." Various conclusions followed from this. A new generation of warhead designers needed to be cultivated. It was desirable to retain a substantial "inactive stockpile of nuclear weapons," of yet undetermined size. And it was necessary to "maintain readiness to resume underground nuclear testing if required."

Along with other military plans and pronouncements, the *Nuclear Posture Review* also made it clear that the Bush administration was committed to two additional controversial policies. One was enhancement of defense against nuclear missiles—which all nuclear nations, including the United States, have always regarded as a threat to their own defense. The other was reluctance to engage in arms-control agreements.[17]

This post-9/11 nuclear assertiveness did not go unchallenged, including from unexpected quarters. In January 2007, four former members of the nuclear priesthood—Henry Kissinger, William Perry, George Shultz, and Sam Nunn—jointly published an essay titled "A World Free of Nuclear Weapons" in the *Wall Street Journal*. This turned out to be prelude to four additional joint essays between 2008 and 2013. The accelerating proliferation of weapons, know-how, and material had brought the world to "a nuclear tipping point," the four men argued, and there was now "a very real possibility that the deadliest weapons ever invented could fall into dangerous hands."[18] In December 2008, more than a hundred world leaders followed up by launching a well-publicized international "Global Zero" campaign in Paris, aimed at phasing out all nuclear warheads by 2030.

President Obama endorsed the Global Zero ideal upon taking office in 2009, and he even earned a Nobel Peace Prize for his rhetoric on nuclear and other global issues. It did not take long, however, for his administration to make clear that complete nuclear disarmament was unattainable. The *Nuclear Posture Review* of April 2010 departed from the previous administration in affirming there would be no nuclear testing and no development of new weapons. That same year, Washington and Moscow concluded a so-called New START Treaty agreeing to further reductions in strategic warheads. The treaty did not contain limits on nonstrategic weapons or non-deployed warheads, however, nor did it affect maintenance of the strategic triad. In a message to the Senate on the New START Treaty, Obama gave assurance that he intended to maintain the nation's rocket-motor industrial base and "modernize or replace the triad of strategic nuclear delivery systems"—that is, heavy bombers and air-launched cruise missiles, land-based intercontinental ballistic missiles, and submarine-launched ballistic missiles.[19]

Instead of becoming another step toward "a world without nuclear weapons"—Obama's words in a celebrated speech in Prague in April—the New START Treaty signaled the victory of post–Cold War strategic planners who advocated a revised paradigm of nuclear deterrence. The huge arsenals that had characterized the balance of terror between the United States and Soviet Union were to be substantially diminished—but not to disappear entirely. Official figures released in March 2015 put the number of deployed strategic warheads at 1,597 for the United States and 1,582 for Russia. (Other sources give slightly higher numbers.)

Considering that the combined nuclear stockpiles of the two superpowers had totaled more than sixty thousand warheads at the peak of the Cold War, this retreat from "mutually assured destruction" was impressive. This accomplishment was undercut, however, by the fact that nine nations now possessed nuclear weapons and none had any serious intention of giving them up. The total number of nuclear-capable countries was very large, and the potential for accidental or deliberate use of these terrible weapons was increasing. The "atomic arc of instability" was even more ominous than when this phrase first came into use a decade earlier.[20]

The Obama administration's concrete long-term nuclear projections were revealed in September 2014. These called for modernizing the nuclear triad by building twelve new ballistic-missile submarines, up to a hundred new long-range bombers, and four hundred new or refurbished land-based ballistic missiles. The forecast even had a phenomenal projected price tag: $355 billion over the next decade, and upwards of $1 trillion over the next thirty years. Much of this projected nuclear force would become fully operative in the 2020s—the very eve, as it happened, of 2030, when the proponents of Global Zero had hoped to see their dream fulfilled.[21]

As of early 2015, nongovernmental sources estimated that the total inventory of nuclear warheads worldwide was around 15,700. Of this number, 4,100 were considered operational, with "about 1,800 U.S. and Russian warheads on high alert." Each of the two nations maintained a reserve of several thousand non-deployed warheads; and each had substantial inventories of retired warheads scheduled for dismantlement (about 3,000 in Russia and 2,500 in the United States). Estimated inventories for the seven other nuclear nations were as follows: France, 300; China, 250; United Kingdom, 215; Pakistan, 100 to 120; India, 90 to 100; Israel, 80; and North Korea, less than 10.[22]

A cover story on "the new nuclear age" published by the *Economist* in March 2015 concluded, "Although there are fewer nuclear weapons than at the height of the cold war . . . the possibility of some of them being used is higher and growing." Russia had committed a third of its military budget to nuclear modernization. China was investing heavily in developing a second-strike capability. Pakistan was focusing on battlefield nuclear weapons to compensate for its inferiority vis-à-vis India in conventional forces (and its military's control over its arsenal was suspect). Both Pakistan and India were developing the ability to deliver such weapons by submarines. North Korea was believed to be developing a missile capable of reaching the West Coast of the United States. Iran was tottering on the verge of joining the nuclear-weapons club (a situation forestalled by conclusion of an agreement with the permanent members of the UN Security Council and the European Union in mid-2015). Should the tipping point tip further, it was speculated that other nations might choose to go nuclear, among them Saudi Arabia, Egypt, Japan, and South Korea.[23]

By the first decade of the twenty-first century, forty-six countries already possessed weapon-usable uranium and thirteen possessed weapon-usable plutonium. According to one very general calculation, this dispersed weapons-grade fissile material was sufficient to make "more than 200,000 nuclear weapons." Add suicidal terrorists intent on buying, stealing, or building a small weapon and smuggling it (like drugs) into a target country and the new balance of nuclear terror was, in its twisted way, as delicate and terrifying as the old one.[24]

CHAPTER 9

THE AMERICAN CENTURY AT SEVENTY-FIVE

2016 marked the seventy-fifth anniversary of "the American century" concept coined by Henry Luce. Had *Life*'s publisher been alive, how might he have responded?

No doubt at one level Luce would have felt his vision of America as "the most powerful and vital nation in the world" had been confirmed. Isolationism was a mindset of the past. World War II had seen to that. "A truly American internationalism" encompassed much of the globe, although rising manifestations of sectarian identity and intolerance were challenging this. "Democratic principles," "freedom under law," "equality of opportunity"—values he extolled as the essence of the Declaration of Independence, Constitution, and Bill of Rights—now had worldwide currency. This was often just rhetoric, but just as often held a place in people's minds and hearts. This had not been the case in 1941, when the most terrible war in modern history was about to engulf the globe.

The spectacle of flourishing consumer societies worldwide would have pleased him greatly. (The 1941 essay had referred to the "more abundant life" that "is characteristically an American promise.") So would have the demise of the Soviet Union. The rise of China, his birthplace and home into his mid-teens, surely would have tormented him: a great culture and long-suffering people at last becoming strong and prosperous, but still under the thumb of atheistic and authoritarian communists.

The "American century" essay reflected a missionary zeal that was literal in Luce's case, son as he was of a Presbyterian family whose life was devoted to spreading the Word to the heathen. Transfigured into patriotism, this zeal amounted to what we today call the gospel of American exceptionalism. In this gospel, Americans surpass all others in virtue and practice—but this can be, and should be, shared. The message was and remains idealistic, generous, moralistic, paternalistic, patronizing, riddled with double standards and hypocrisy, and notably lacking in self-reflection or self-criticism. In that regard, the Henry Luce of 1941 would have found the righteous certainty and missionary rhetoric of his country seventy-five years later familiar and probably comforting. The Cold War and subsequent war on terror heightened such nationalistic oratory, but its roots are deep.

No one writing in 1941, however, could have anticipated the exponential acceleration of change that took place after World War II. And no one who died in 1967, as Luce did, could have imagined how America would emerge from the Vietnam War (which he fervently supported) so tarnished and humiliated, or how the digital revolution would transform the world, extending to military affairs, or how the historical precedent of clashes between nations would be followed by an epoch of nonstate and irregular violence and terror that succeeded in making fear itself a bedrock feature of both America and the American century.

There is no way of knowing how the man who wrote in 1941 that it was "emphatically" not America's mission "to undertake to police the whole world" would have responded to the CIA and elite US special operations forces carrying out covert missions in around 150 nations—or to the United States utilizing upwards of eight hundred overseas military bases. What would he have said about annual US military spending in the neighborhood of $1 trillion and the Pentagon's annual "base budget" being greater than the next eight nations combined? Or about a military establishment whose mission was now defined as maintaining full-spectrum dominance not only on land, in the air, and on the sea but also in outer space and cyberspace? Or about the fact that the United States was the largest supplier of weapons worldwide, accounting for close to half of all arms transfers by value between 2007 and 2014?[1]

Given his ideological hostility to "collectivism" of even the New Deal sort, we can only guess what Luce might have said about his country's transformation into a national security state and a surveillance state. In all likelihood, he would have applauded resisting thoroughgoing nuclear disarmament and endorsed the modernization of America's reduced arsenal, but even this cannot be said for sure. Many members of the Cold War nuclear priesthood, after all, ultimately came to see nuclear deterrence as folly in an age of global fragmentation.

It is not difficult to imagine Luce being astonished and confounded by the chaos of the twenty-first century, which differed so greatly from the titanic collision of nations and ideologies that prompted him to write his hopeful vision of an impending American century in 1941. Seventy-five years afterwards he would have found his beloved country mired militarily in two small nations, Afghanistan and Iraq, in conflicts that already had lasted more than three times as long as the interval between Pearl Harbor and the end of World War II. Beyond this, the US military was simultaneously engaged in conflicts in five other countries in the Greater Middle East (Pakistan, Syria, Libya, Yemen, and Somalia), again with no end in sight.

At first glance, these place names might have suggested a semblance of continuity with the nation-state conflicts of the past, but this impression would have disappeared quickly. The country names merely papered over a crazy quilt of patron states and proxy wars, surrogate forces, insurgencies, rival terrorist and militia organizations, sectarian hatreds, tribal and ethnic conflicts, and flat-out crime and corruption. No ordinary onlooker could have been expected to spell out who was fighting whom.

In official accounts, the Iraq and Afghan wars both ended before 2016. The United States announced the withdrawal of its combat forces from Iraq in December 2011, and two years later President Obama declared that America was no longer pursuing a "global war on terror" per se. In 2014, both the United States and NATO formally terminated their combat missions in Afghanistan. These were significant operational as well as symbolic developments, but in actual practice they did not end military intervention in the two beleaguered countries—nor did they end the activity there of many thousands of American and foreign private contractors on the Pentagon's payroll. The old war-on-terror campaign continued in new circumstances under new names.[2]

US-led foreign forces never completely withdrew from Afghanistan at all. As of mid-2016, close to 7,000 American military personnel were training and otherwise assisting Afghan troops; another 2,850 in-country US special operations forces were engaged in covert "counter-terrorism" missions; more than 5,850 NATO soldiers were deployed in Afghanistan; and the number of military contractors numbered at least 26,000. In Iraq, US military personnel began returning in mid-2014 in response to the emergence there and in neighboring Syria of the militant Islamic State of Iraq and Syria (ISIS), an organization that traced back to opposition to the US-led invasion of 2003. ISIS had routed US-trained Iraqi government forces from key cities beginning early in 2014 and in June audaciously declared itself a caliphate. By mid-2016, the number of US forces in Iraq was around 5,000, including special operations units and aircraft engaged in bombing missions in both Iraq and Syria. Between August 2014 and April 2016, air strikes operating in and outside Iraq dropped more than 40,000 bombs.[3]

In Syria, which had imploded in brutal civil war in 2011, ISIS's depredations exacerbated an already anarchic arena of death and destruction in which the Syrian government, backed by Iran as well as by Russian warplanes, bombarded densely populated rebel-held urban areas with munitions ranging from crude barrel bombs to incendiaries and phosphorus bombs, cluster bombs, huge "bunker busters," and chlorine-gas attacks. Estimates of the number of rebels, civilians, and government forces killed after five years of strife were around half a million, and great cities like Aleppo lay in ruins. In a nation whose prewar population was around 22 to 23 million, at least 6.6 million were internally displaced and some 4.9 million had fled and become refugees. These uprooted individuals—amounting to half of the country's prewar population—were, of course, but a portion of the more than 65 million people forcibly displaced worldwide that the United Nations reported on early in 2016.

Imagining what Henry Luce might have thought seventy-five

years after his famous essay appeared is a game, of course, but one that can help sharpen past and present in intimate, provocative ways. By 2016, America's militaristic response to 9/11 was fifteen years old and had undergone various name changes—from "GWOT" to "overseas contingency operations" (a bureaucratic rechristening in 2009, for budgetary purposes) to "the long war" (common in military circles) and even "the forever war" (in critical popular commentaries). Persuasive cumulative data was on hand as never before, and it is hard to imagine Luce not finding much of this startling and disturbing: the tragic number of displaced persons worldwide, surpassed only by World War II and its immediate aftermath; the extremely high incidence of long-term mental and emotional disorders among veterans of America's postwar wars, including even the supposedly low-casualty Gulf War of 1991; the political harm done to democracy by creating a gargantuan national security state devoted to perpetuating a state of semi-war; the huge fiscal costs that had been incurred for decades to come by a hubristic and disproportionate response to a single day of terror.

At the same time, however, Luce also surely would have pointed out that much of the violence tearing the Greater Middle East apart had indigenous roots. No one could seriously deny this—but neither could any serious observer deny that Washington's (and London's) reckless responses to September 11 were a major trigger of this destabilization and disintegration. The irony of the situation was that much of the official rhetoric that accompanied the launching of the disastrous war on terror had sounded like a crib from his own 1941 articulation of America's mission and manifest destiny.

Where London was concerned, in 2016 Luce would have had access to that year's publication of the thirteen-volume "Chilcot report," conveying the results of a seven-year-long inquiry into British involvement in the invasion and occupation of Iraq. The report was a devastating indictment of both the government's decision to join the United States in launching preemptive war and the British military's ineptitude in defining and performing its mission. Luce might (but probably would not) have asked why no comparable official inquiry empowered to subpoena documents, mobilize testimony, evaluate decision-making, and assess individual and institutional accountability was ever undertaken in the United States. Actually, the sharper question is why such an undertaking is politically impossible in America. Is unaccountability integral to exceptionalism?[4]

There is no reason to imagine that, observing all this violence and suffering—and all the mayhem and bloodshed after 1945 that preceded it—Luce's faith in America as the world's last, best hope would have been shaken. It is easy to picture him joining the chorus of detached observers who argue that violence has been contained compared to the horrors of World War II and earlier times—and that even the death, pain, and agony we have seen since September 11 actually reflects, on the part of the United States, a praiseworthy technological and psychological turn in the direction of precision, restraint, and concern with avoiding civilian casualties.

The mystique of exceptional virtue does not accommodate serious consideration of irresponsibility, provocation, intoxication with brute force, paranoia, hubris, reckless and criminal actions, or even criminal negligence.

Notes

Chapter 1: Measuring Violence

1   General Martin Dempsey to the Senate Armed Services Committee in February 2013; he spoke similarly to the House Armed Services Committee the next day, and also in 2012 testimony.

2   Steven Pinker, *The Better Angels of Our Nature: Why Violence Has Declined* (Penguin, 2011), xxi. Online commentary by and about Pinker is voluminous. He acknowledges adopting the "Long Peace" label from the historian John Gaddis. The "most peaceable era" quote appears in the first paragraph of his book, and is repeated in essentially the same words in many of his presentations. The declinist argument was, in fact, well established before Pinker's book. A scholarly review published in 2003, for example, observed that "it has become almost commonplace to say that war is becoming obsolete." See Meredith Reid Sarkees, Frank Whelon Wayman, and J. David Singer, "Inter-State, Intra-State, and Extra-State Wars: A Comprehensive Look at Their Distribution over Time, 1816–1997," *International Studies Quarterly* 47 (2003): 49–70.

3   See the tables compiled by Genocide Watch: The International Alliance to End Genocide, in "Genocides, Politicides, and Other Mass Murder Since 1945" (2010), at genocidewatch.org. Their

"cumulative civilian death" totals are rounded off and do not give high/low estimates.

4   This is widely quoted. See, for example, Steven Pinker and Andrew Mack, "The World Is Not Falling Apart," *Slate*, December 22, 2014.

5   United Nations High Commissioner for Refugees (UNHCR), *Global Trends: Forced Displacement in 2015* (June 2016). For earlier reports, see *UNHCR: Mid-Year Trends 2015* and UNHCR, *Global Trends: Forced Displacement in 2014*.

6   David Rieff, "Were Sanctions Right?" *New York Times Magazine*, July 27, 2003.

7   "Minefield: Mental Health in the Middle East," *Economist*, May 21, 2016.

8   Terri Tanielian and Lisa H. Jaycox, ed., *Invisible Wounds of War: Psychological and Cognitive Injuries, Their Consequences, and Services to Assist Recovery* (RAND Center for Military Health Policy Research, 2008), especially pages xxi, 3–5. See also chapter 7 in this present book for later data on PTSD, TBI, and related mental disorders.

9   Institute for Economics and Peace, *Global Terrorism Index 2015* (November 2015), at economicsandpeace.org; Chicago Project on Security and Terrorism (CPOST), "Suicide Attack Database" (updated April 19, 2016), at cpostdata.uchicago.edu.

10   For a concise reprise of this argument by the director of the Belfer Center for Science and International Affairs at Harvard Kennedy School of Government, see Graham Allison, "Fear Death from Tree Limbs, Not Terrorists," *Boston Globe*, February 22, 2016.

11   For the "three Ds," Scott Atran quotes an unnamed air force general as follows: "I was trained for Ds—defeat, destroy, devastate—now I'm told we have responsibility for the Rs—rebuild, reform, renew. Well, I was never trained for that, so what the Hell am I supposed to do? Destroy in just the right way to rebuild?" Quoted in Atran's "Pathways to and from Violent Extremism: The Case for Science-Based Field Research," a presentation before the Senate Armed Services Subcommittee on Emerging Threats and Capabilities," March 3, 2010. "Full-spectrum dominance" and other slogans and mission statements are addressed below in chapter 6. The "full spectrum" mantra was introduced in two Joint Chiefs of

Staff publications: *Joint Vision 2010* (1996) and *Joint Vision 2020* (2000). The Air Force Global Strike Command was activated in 2009 as the successor to the Cold War–era Strategic Air Command (inactivated in 1992), following several alarming incidents involving the mishandling of nuclear weapons. For overseas bases, see Department of Defense, *Base Structure Report—Fiscal Year 2015 Baseline* (especially page DoD-6). For the unofficial count (around eight hundred bases in eighty countries), see David Vine, "The United States Probably Has More Foreign Military Bases Than Any Other People, Nation, or Empire in History," *Nation*, September 14, 2015; also Vine's in-depth study *Base Nation: How U.S. Bases Abroad Harm America and the World* (Metropolitan Books/Henry Holt, 2015), which includes attention to "lily pad" facilities that come and go. The overseas deployment of Special Operation Forces is addressed below in chapter 8. Nick Turse is the major investigator publishing on this subject, often on the *TomDispatch* website (TomDispatch.com). In 2016, William D. Hartung calculated that the United States "is contributing to the arming and training of security forces in 180 countries"; see his "The Pentagon's War on Accountability" on *TomDispatch*, May 24, 2016.

12   Regularly updated data on US drone strikes, focusing on Pakistan, Yemen, and Somalia, are accessible on the Bureau of Investigative Journalism website (thebureauinvestigates.com). Updated British drone strikes are tabulated on the Drone Wars UK website. On deadly Israeli drone strikes in Gaza in 2014, see Ann Wright, "Two Years Ago Israel Attacked Gaza for 51 Days as Drone Warfare Becomes the Norm," June 8, 2016, on the *Alternet* website (alternet.org).

13   Stockholm International Peace Research Institute, "Global Nuclear Weapons: Downsizing but Modernizing," June 13, 2016, accessible at the sipri.org website.

14   Alan Robock and Owen Brian Toon, "Let's End the Peril of a Nuclear Winter," *New York Times*, February 11, 2016; also their earlier "Local Nuclear War, Global Suffering," *Scientific American* 302 (January 2010), 74–81. The authors are scientists involved in nuclear-winter research. "Nuclear weapons capable" nations are discussed in chapters 2 and 8.

15   For a concise summary of US nuclear weapons and the modernization agenda, see Hans M. Kristensen and Robert Norris, "United States Nuclear Forces, 2016," *Bulletin of the Atomic Scientists* 72, no. 2 ("Nuclear Notebook"), March 2016, 63–73.

16   The eight nations, not identified in the president's speech, are as follows (in descending order of annual defense spending): China, Russia, Saudi Arabia, France, United Kingdom, Germany, Japan, and India. See Anthony H. Cordesman, *The FY2016 Defense Budget and US Strategy: Key Trends and Data Points* (Center for Strategic and International Studies, March 2, 2015), 3–12, especially the table on page 12 based on data for 2014 compiled by the Stockholm International Peace Research Institute. The Defense Department's annual base budget given here is $640 billion; for the next eight nations combined it is $607 billion.

17   For a tabular breakdown of the $1 trillion budget, based on government sources, see Mandy Smithberger, "Pentagon's 2017 Budget Was Mardi Gras for Defense Contractors," *Defense Monitor*, January–March 2016, accessible at the Project on Government Oversight (pogoarchives.org). Melvin Goodman presents a critical historical examination of post–World War II US military spending in *National Insecurity: The Cost of American Militarism* (City Lights, 2013). See also William D. Hartung, "The Pentagon's War on Accountability," *TomDispatch*, May 24, 2016.

18   Luce's three mass-circulation magazines—*Time*, *Life*, and *Fortune*—had a strong impact on public opinion, and Luce exercised considerable but not total influence over their political slant. For a well-documented overview, see Alan Brinkley, *The Publisher: Henry Luce and His American Century* (Knopf, 2009).

19   Brinkley, *The Publisher*, chapter 12 ("Cold Warriors"). See especially pages 365, 367, 377, 445–47 (turning the Korean and Vietnam conflicts into war with China), and 366, 372–73, 375–76 (preemptive use of nuclear weapons against the Soviet Union and China).

20   See, for example, the various evaluations in Andrew Bacevich, ed., *The Short American Century: A Postmortem* (Harvard University Press, 2012).

Chapter 2: Legacies of World War II

1   Department of Veterans Affairs, "America's Wars," May 2015, at va.gov. No detail is given for the category "Other deaths in service (Non-Theater)," a standard and large category that begins in the Spanish-American War of 1898–1902.

2   George Orwell used the term "Cold War" in an October 1945 essay titled "You and the Atom Bomb," but mainstreaming the label is commonly attributed to a speech by Bernard Baruch in April 1947 that was picked up and popularized by Walter Lippmann and other journalists.

3   B. V. A. Röling, "The Tokyo Trial and the Quest for Peace," in *The Tokyo War Crimes Trial: An International Symposium*, ed., C. Hosoya et al. (Kodansha and Kodansha International, 1986), 130.

4   Richard Overy, "Total War II: The Second World War," in *The Oxford Illustrated History of Modern War*, ed., Charles Townshend (Oxford University Press, 1997), 129–31; see also Overy's chapter on "Air Warfare" in ibid.

5   Emergence of the US policy of targeting civilian populations is traced in detail in chapter 8 ("Air War and Terror Bombing in World War II") in John W. Dower, *Cultures of War: Pearl Harbor / Hiroshima / 9-11 / Iraq* (Norton and New Press, 2010).

6   For a short summary used by the US National Museum of World War II, see David Mindell, "The Science and Technology of World War II," accessible on the learnnc.org website.

Chapter 3: Cold War Nuclear Terror

1   This contradiction is addressed in Tom Engelhardt, *The End of Victory Culture*, updated 2nd ed. (University of Massachusetts Press, 2009; originally published in 1995).

2   The "madman theory" received considerable attention beginning around 1998, and secret documents on Operation Duck Hook were declassified in November 2005. See especially the following: William Burr and Jeffrey P. Kimball, ed., "Nixon White House Considered Nuclear Options Against North Vietnam, Declassified Documents Reveal: Nuclear Weapons, the Vietnam War, and the 'Nuclear Taboo,'" National Security Archive, July

31, 2006, accessible at the nsarchive.gwu.edu website; Burr and Kimball, *Nixon's Nuclear Specter: The Secret Alert of 1969, Madman Diplomacy, and the Vietnam War* (University of Kansas Press, 2015); Robert G. Kaiser, "The Disaster of Richard Nixon," *New York Review of Books*, April 21, 2016; H. R. Haldeman, *The Ends of Power* (Times Books, 1978; quoted in Kaiser, "Disaster of Richard Nixon"); Scott D. Sagan and Jeremi Suri, "The Madman Nuclear Alert: Secrecy, Signaling, and Safety in October 1969," *International Security* 27, no. 4 (Spring 2003): 150–83. The last of these sources uses the madman theory as a case study to test the political science literature on "nuclear weapons diplomacy."

3   The declassified text of NSC 162/2 ("A Report to the National Security Council by the Executive Secretary on Basic National Security Policy," October 30, 1953) is accessible on the Federation of American Scientists website (hereafter fas.org).

4   Albert Wohlstetter, "The Delicate Balance of Terror," *Foreign Affairs*, January 1959.

5   The somewhat redacted SAC document was released in 2015, with useful summary commentary, by the National Security Archive at George Washington University. See William Burr, ed., "U.S. Cold War Nuclear Target Lists Declassified for First Time," National Security Archive Electronic Briefing Book No. 538, accessible at nsarchive.gwu.edu.

6   The physicist Wm. Robert Johnston has compiled a wide-ranging "Nuclear Weapons" archive within his sprawling "Johnston's Archive" website at johnstonsarchive.net. The key tables covering the nuclear arms race are sourced in considerable part from estimates by the National Resource Defense Council and the *Bulletin of the Atomic Scientists*. Johnston's tables include timelines beginning in 1945, distinguish between strategic and nonstrategic warheads, and also provide megatonnage for the US and Soviet/Russian arsenals. They are accessible in a section titled "Nuclear stockpiles: Cumulative estimates." See also Hans M. Kristensen and Robert S. Norris, "Global Nuclear Weapons Inventories, 1945–2013," *Bulletin of the Atomic Scientists* 69, no. 5 (September–October, 2013). The cumulative table on page 76 of this overview covers US and Soviet stockpiles through 2013, but with no breakdown between strategic and tactical warheads.

Estimated arsenals vary somewhat depending on the source. The numbers in the text here follow Johnston's useful breakdowns.

7   Joint Chiefs of Staff, "Memorandum for the Secretary of Defense: Berlin Contingency Planning," June 26, 1961, especially pages 1–5, 20. (This fifty-three-page memo gives fatality projections in percentages, which I have applied to the Soviet and Chinese populations as of 1960.) The memo was declassified for the National Security Archive at George Washington University in November 2011 and is accessible online. For nuclear targeting of China, see Hans M. Kristensen, Robert S. Norris, and Matthew G. McKinzie, *Chinese Nuclear Forces and U.S. Nuclear Planning* (Federation of American Scientists and Natural Resources Defense Council, November 2006), especially chapter 3 ("China in U.S. Nuclear War Planning"), 127–72, accessible at fas.org. Eric Schlosser provides vivid archives-based details of the paranoid extremism of US nuclear planning in his excellent study *Command and Control: Nuclear Weapons, the Damascus Accident, and the Illusion of Safety* (Penguin Press, 2013); see especially pages 202–7 (the 1960–61 genesis of SIOP, the ultrasecret and regularly updated Single Integrated Operational Plan that essentially defined nuclear targets until the early twenty-first century) and 351–56 (apocalyptic secret projections of the devastating impact of all-out nuclear attacks).

8   The total tonnage of all bombs dropped by US and British air forces in World War II was close to 3.4 million, with the typical conventional bomb carrying a payload equivalent to one ton of TNT. The 1954 Bikini test that irradiated a Japanese fishing boat triggered the belated development of the antinuclear movement in postwar Japan.

9   Kristensen and Norris, "Global Nuclear Weapons Inventories, 1945–2013." For a full list of US nuclear tests, see US Department of Energy, Nevada Operations Office, *United States Nuclear Tests: July 1945 through September 1992*, December 2000; this 185-page report is accessible at nnsa.energy.gov.

10   See the tables in Johnston, "Nuclear Stockpiles."

11   Amy F. Woolf, *U.S. Strategic Nuclear Forces: Background, Developments, and Issues* (Congressional Research Service, March 18, 2015), accessible at fas.org.

12   The key secondary sources on US overseas deployment of
nuclear weapons, based on declassified US documents, are as
follows: 1) Two articles in the *Bulletin of the Atomic Scientists* by
Robert S. Norris, William M. Arkin, and William Burr: "Where
They Were," (November/December 1999), 26–35, and "Where
They Were: How Much Did Japan Know?" (January/February
2000), 11–13, 78–79. 2) Robert S. Norris, "United States Nuclear
Weapons Deployments Abroad, 1950–1977," Carnegie Endowment for International Peace (November 30, 1999). I have used
the illuminating "Pacific Ashore" table in this presentation for
some of the numbers cited in these paragraphs. 3) Hans Kristensen, *Japan Under the US Nuclear Umbrella* (Nautilus Institute
for Security and Sustainability, July 1999), at nautilus.org.

13   S. L. Simon and W. L. Robinson, "A Compilation of Nuclear
Weapons Test Detonation Data for U.S. Pacific Ocean Tests,"
Health Physics 73 (July 1997): 258–64.

14   For the State Department's measured evaluation of the treaty's
effect, see Office of the Historian, "Milestones: 1961–1968—The
Limited Test Ban Treaty, 1963," accessible on the history.state.gov
website. China and France did not sign the NPT until 1992. The
NPT paved the way for subsequent arms-control negotiations,
most notably the Strategic Arms Limitations Talks (SALT I) that
began in 1969 and led, among other agreements, to a bilateral
Anti-Ballistic Missile Treaty in 1972.

15   On nuclear-capable states, see Arms Control Association, "The
Status of the Comprehensive Test Ban Treaty: Signatories and
Ratifiers," March 2014, on their website armscontrol.org, which
lists forty-four such states, of which thirty-six had ratified the
CTBT. See also the tabular presentations (especially figure 1.1
and table 1.1) in *Universal Compliance: A Strategy for Nuclear
Security* (Carnegie Endowment for International Peace, June
2007), accessed at carnegieendowment.org. For additional detail,
see chapters 2 and 8.

16   The "nuclear taboo" concept amounts to a corrective or comple-
ment to so-called realist arguments that posit deterrence
thinking as the key to avoiding nuclear war. The major study is
Nina Tannenwald, *The Nuclear Taboo: The United States and the
Non-Use of Nuclear Weapons since 1945* (Cambridge University

Press, 2007). She also presents her argument in an earlier article: "Stigmatizing the Bomb: Origins of the Nuclear Taboo," *International Security* 29, no. 4 (2005): 5–49.

17   "General Lee Butler's Speech and His Joint Statement with General Goodpaster," December 4, 1996, transcript on the pbs. org website of PBS's "American Experience"; Robert Green, "On Serendipity, Enlightened Leadership and Persistence," review of Butler's self-published memoir *Uncommon Cause: A Life at Odds with Convention* (2015); Robert Kazel, "General Lee Butler to Nuclear Abolition Movement: 'Don't Give Up,'" interview conducted in 2015. Both of the latter two citations are accessible on the wagingpeace.org website, which includes many other quotable Butler presentations.

18   William J. Perry, *My Life at the Nuclear Brink* (Stanford University Press, 2015), especially pages 35, 55.

19   Schlosser, *Command and Control*, 327. For a long review of Schlosser's incisive study of actual and potential nuclear ac cidents, see Louis Menard, "Nukes of Hazard," *New Yorker*, September 30, 2013.

20   Seth Baum, "Nuclear War, the Black Swan We Can Never See," *Bulletin of the Atomic Scientists*, November 21, 2014. A more focused "timeline of close calls" describes twenty-six incidents between 1956 and 2010, of which twenty-three took place between 1956 and 1983 (nine of them during the Cuban Missile Crisis of October 1962); see "Accidental Nuclear War: A Timeline of Close Calls," on the futureoflife.org website.

21   The air crash over Palomares received lengthy coverage in the *New York Times* a half-century later. See Dave Philipps, "Decades Later, Sickness Among Airmen After a Hydrogen Bomb Accident," *New York Times*, June 19, 2016, and Raphael Minder, "Even Without Blast, 4 Hydrogen Bombs from '66 Scar Spanish Village," *New York Times*, June 20, 2016. The 1966 incident calls attention to the larger issue of American "atomic veterans" and "downwinders" who were exposed to radiation during US nuclear tests as well as cleanup operations like the one that followed the Palomares accident.

22   Peter Hayes and Nina Tannenwald, "Nixing Nukes in Vietnam," *Bulletin of the Atomic Scientists*, May–June, 2003. See also Tan-

nenwald, *The Nuclear Taboo*. The declassified secret *Tactical Nuclear Weapons in Southeast Asia* report is accessible on several websites.

Chapter 4: Cold War Wars

1   Of the 3.4 million tons of bombs dropped by the US and British air forces in World War II, 654,400 tons were dropped in the Pacific theater and the rest in Europe. In the US air raids that destroyed sixty-four Japanese cities prior to Hiroshima and Nagasaki, total tonnage dropped was 160,800 tons (24 percent of the Pacific theater total); U.S. Strategic Bombing Survey, *Summary Report (Pacific War)*, July 1, 1946, 16. Bruce Cumings puts the tonnage dropped on Korea at 667,557 tons (including 32,557 tons of napalm); *The Korean War: A History* (Modern Library, 2010), 159. LeMay's blunt observation appears in Curtis E. LeMay with MacKinlay Kantor, *Mission with LeMay: My Story* (Doubleday, 1960), 382.

2   The usual estimate for bombs dropped by the United States on Vietnam, Cambodia, and Laos is seven million tons. For Kissinger's quote, see Elizabeth Becker, "Kissinger Tapes Describe Crises, War and Stark Photos of Abuse," *New York Times*, May 27, 2004. Engelhardt's comment appears at his website *TomDispatch*, June 7, 2016.

3   For a concise genealogy of Agent Orange beginning in World War II and extending through the Korean War and Malayan Emergency to the Vietnam War, see Judith Perera and Andy Thomas, "This Horrible Natural Experiment," *New Scientist*, April 18, 1985. Long-term illnesses and disabilities suffered by American Vietnam War veterans as a consequence of exposure to Agent Orange, including possible birth defects in offspring, are recognized by the Department of Veterans Affairs under the rubric of war-related "presumptive diseases."

4   Alex P. Schmid and Ellen Berends, *Soviet Military Interventions since 1945* (Transaction Books, 1985). The authors identify forty-four loosely defined Soviet "interventions," but focus on only a small number of case studies. Apart from the episodes

mentioned, plus the final fatal intervention in Afghanistan, these include a "nonintervention" in the Greek civil war (1944–49), Iran (1945–46), the occupation of Austria (1945–55), and the Korean War (1950–53). Wikipedia's "List of wars 1945–1989" details the Soviet Union as a participant in the following ten "wars": East Germany (1953), Hungary (1956), Eritrea (1961), Czechoslovakia (1968), Sino-Soviet border conflict (1969), Indo-Pakistani War (1971, backing India), Ethiopian civil war (1974-91), Angolan Civil War (1975–2002), Ethio-Somali War (1977–78, backing Ethiopia), Afghanistan (1979–89).

5   Ahmed Rashid, "Pakistan: Worse Than We Knew," *New York Review of Books*, June 5, 2014.

6   Even while supporting Iraq in the Iran-Iraq War, in 1985 and 1986 the United States engaged in a clandestine deal to sell more than two thousand anti-tank and anti-aircraft missiles to Iran via Israel. Soon exposed and publicized as the "Iran-Contra affair," the US hope was (1) to persuade Iran to release seven American hostages it held, and (2) to use the proceeds from the weapons sale to fund right-wing "Contras" fighting the left-wing Sandinista government in Nicaragua.

7   The difficulty of estimating total combatant and noncombatant fatalities in the Korean, Vietnam, and Soviet-Afghanistan wars can be gleaned from Wikipedia's lengthy annotated entries; see "Civilian casualty ratio," "Korean War," "Vietnam War," "Vietnam War casualties," and "Soviet war in Afghanistan." On the Iran-Iraq war, see Charles Kurzman, "Death Tolls of the Iran-Iraq War," October 31, 2013, posted at kurzmanunc.edu. Kurzman provides crosslinks to major sources for fatality estimates, and suggests that census data indicates the actual total may have been less than even the relatively low official Iraqi and Iranian estimates. Definitional and quantitative issues are addressed in Bethany Lacina and Nils Petter Gleditsch, "Monitoring Trends in Global Conflict: A New Dataset of Battle Deaths," *European Journal of Population* 21 (2005): 145–66.

8   Wikipedia's entry on "Chinese Civil War," for example, employs the evasive term "casualties" rather than "fatalities," citing a total of "6 million (including civilians)" for the 1945–1949 period. An analysis of "battle deaths" that includes under this rubric "all

people, soldiers and civilians, killed in combat," or in the course
of "military operations," puts the estimate at 1.2 million; Lacina
and Gleditsch, "Monitoring Trends in Global Conflict," 154.

9   The Convention on the Prevention and Punishment of the
Crime of Genocide (CPPCG) adopted by the United Nations
in 1948 defines genocide as "acts committed with the intent to
destroy, in whole or in part, a national, ethnic, racial, or religious
group." Resolution 96 introduced in the UN in December 1946
identified "crimes of genocide" as occurring "when racial, religious, political and other groups have been destroyed, entirely or
in part." The deletion of "political" in the CPPCG followed pressure from the Soviet Union and some other nations, but many
scholars and political activists continue to defer to the original
1946 definition; see, for example, Ervin Staub, *The Roots of Evil:
The Origins of Genocide and Other Group Violence* (Cambridge
University Press, 1989), 8. This is why many lists of post-1945
genocides include political mass murders that have taken place
in countries like China, the former Soviet Union, Cambodia,
Indonesia, and North Korea. Some watchdog groups devoted to
curbing genocide take care to title their reports to make explicitly clear that political murders are included. See, for example,
The International Alliance to End Genocide, "Genocides, Politicides, and Other Mass Murder Since 1945" (c. 2010), accessible
at the genocidewatch.org website. Present-day listings identify
as many as thirty or more postwar incidents as genocidal. See,
for example, Inter-Parliamentary Alliance for Human Rights and
Global Peace (IPAHP), "Acts of Genocide since World War II"
(c. 2014), on the ipahp.org website.

10   Monty G. Marshall, comp., "Major Episodes of Political Violence,
1946–2013," Center for Systemic Peace, Virginia; accessible on
the systemicpeace.org website. The CIA funding is acknowledged in the endnotes to this detailed list, which was updated on
March 27, 2014.

11   Meredith Reid Sarkees, Frank Whelon Wayman, and J. David
Singer, "Inter-State, Intra-State, and Extra-State Wars: A Comprehensive Look at Their Distribution over Time, 1816–1997,"
International Studies Quarterly 47, no. 1 (2003): 49–70. This article provides a detailed analysis of the Correlates of War Project

data and methodology.

12   The Uppsala criteria for "war" is a thousand battle-related deaths in a calendar year. See Lotta Themner and Peter Walensteen, "Armed Conflict, 1946–2013," *Journal of Peace Research* 51, no. 4 (2014) for access to UCDP data as well as clarification of key terms and concepts governing the quantification.

13   The quotation appears in Richard F. Grimmett, "Instances of Use of United States Armed Forces Abroad, 1798–2004," Congressional Research Service (report RL30172), October 5, 2004; accessed at the Naval Historical Center website at au.af.mil. This CRS report was updated (as RL32170) by Grimmett on January 27, 2010, to cover the years 1798–2009, and updated again (as RL42738) on October 7, 2016, by Barbara Salazar Torreon to cover 1798–2016. The most recent version is accessible at fas.org.

14   "Covert Operations," at the Global Security website (globalsecurity.org) provides descriptive commentary on eighty-one covert operations. See also William Blum, "A Brief History of U.S. Interventions: 1945 to the Present," *Z Magazine*, June 1999, which focuses on thirty-two interventions. In *Killing Hope: US Military and CIA Interventions Since World War II* (Common Courage Press, 1995), Blum calls attention to seventy "extremely serious interventions." See also Tim Weiner, *Legacy of Ashes: The History of the CIA* (Doubleday, 2007). As his title suggests, Weiner is critical of the CIA, albeit as much for its incompetence as for its engagement in reprehensible activities.

15   The original OSS booklet *Simple Sabotage Field Manual* was declassified by the CIA in 2012 and is widely accessible online. The illustrated sabotage pamphlet prepared by the CIA for distribution in Nicaragua is discussed in chapter 5.

16   Operation CHAOS was terminated in 1973 and publicly disclosed in a lengthy article by Seymour Hersh, "Huge C.I.A. Operation Reported in U.S. Against Antiwar Forces, Other Dissidents in Nixon Years," *New York Times*, December 22, 1974. Surveillance eventually extended to around a thousand organizations.

17   Coleman McCarthy, "The Consequences of Covert Tactics," *Washington Post*, December 13, 1987. The group's name was the Association for Responsible Dissent and its director was John Stockwell, who had been a CIA operative in Angola, the Congo,

and Vietnam, and who at one point sat in on a subcommittee of the National Security Agency. In the mid-1980s, Stockwell delivered a long public talk at various venues titled "Secret Wars of the CIA," accessible online in various forms. The vague estimate of six million fatalities due to CIA operations quoted by the *Washington Post* appears to include complicity in major bloodlettings such as the Vietnam War and the massacre of alleged communists in Indonesia in 1965–66.

18   The key passage in Carter's State of the Union address is as follows: "The region which is now threatened by Soviet troops in Afghanistan is of great strategic importance: It contains more than two-thirds of the world's exportable oil. The Soviet effort to dominate Afghanistan has brought Soviet military forces to within 300 miles of the Indian Ocean and close to the Straits [*sic*] of Hormuz, a waterway through which most of the world's oil must flow. The Soviet Union is now attempting to consolidate a strategic position, therefore, that poses a grave threat to the free movement of Middle East oil." Later in this address, Carter noted that "the crises in Iran and Afghanistan have dramatized a very important lesson: Our excessive dependence on foreign oil is a clear and present danger to our Nation's security." The Carter Doctrine was drafted largely by Zbigniew Brzezinski, the president's national security adviser.

19   Michael A. Palmer, "The Navy: The Transoceanic Period, 1945–1992," a section in "History of the U.S. Navy," (n.d.) on the Naval History and Heritage Command website (history.navy.mil).

20   For Brzezinski's account of the anti-Soviet operation in Afghanistan, see "Interview with Dr. Zbigniew Brzezinski (13/6/97)," at nsarchive.gwu.edu.

21   Ronald Reagan, "PEACE: Restoring the Margin of Safety," address to the Veterans of Foreign Wars convention in Chicago, August 18, 1980. This is accessible through the Reagan Library (reaganlibrary.archives.gov) and also at The American Presidency Project website of the University of California, Santa Barbara (presidency.ucsb.edu). The "Vietnam syndrome" argument, cherished in conservative circles to the present day, ignored several things. One was the atrocious nature of US war conduct in Vietnam that television and investigative reporting brought

into American homes on a daily basis. Another was the drumbeat of reported American battle deaths that continued year after year—compounded by the psychological damage the conflict inflicted on many of those who survived. A third was the steady drip of revelations about the corruption and venality of the South Vietnamese governments on whose behalf the United States was presumably fighting. As the war dragged on, discipline and morale among US fighting forces eroded, leading to rising discord and apprehension of disintegration within the military establishment itself. To all this must be added the unanticipated tenacity and resilience of the Vietnamese enemy, both North Vietnamese soldiers and National Liberation Front (Viet Cong) forces in the South.

22   Greg Schneider and Renae Merle, "Reagan's Defense Buildup Bridged Military Eras: Huge Budgets Brought Life Back to Industry," *Washington Post*, June 9, 2004.

23   "Launching the Missile That Made History," *Wall Street Journal*, October 1, 2011.

24   Francis X. Clines, "Military of U.S. 'Standing Tall,' Reagan Asserts," *New York Times*, December 13, 1983. A short army publication on the invasion of Grenada published a quarter century later reiterates this celebration of escaping the bleak shadow of Vietnam. A sentence in its concluding paragraph states that despite problems of interservice collaboration, "The operation achieved its goals and served as a symbol to the services and to the world that the United States had begun to recover from the 'Vietnam syndrome.'" *Operation Urgent Fury: The Invasion of Grenada, October 1983* (U.S. Army Center of Military History, 2008), 36.

Chapter 5: Proxy War and Surrogate Terror

1   John H. Coatsworth, "The Cold War in Central America, 1979–1991," in Melvyn Lefler and Odd Arne Westad, ed., *The Cambridge History of the Cold War*, vol. 3 (Cambridge, 2010), 220.

2   "Alleged Assassination Plots Involving Foreign Leaders," interim report of the Select Committee to Study Governmental Opera-

tions with Respect to Intelligence Activities, US Senate (1975), 71. The committee is better known as the "Church Committee," after its chair, Senator Frank Church.

3   Timothy J. Kepner, "Torture 101: The Case Against the United States for Atrocities Committed by the School of the Americas," *Dickinson Journal of International Law* 19 (Spring 2001). This taps the voluminous critical literature on the SOA. In 1996, an Amnesty International film festival in Amsterdam featured a documentary on SOA titled "Inside the School of the Assassins." For another lawyerly prosecution brief, see Bill Quigley, "The Case for Closing the School of the Americas," *Brigham Young University Journal of Public Law* 20, no. 1 (May 2005).

4   For a close analysis that places US support of Operation Condor in the larger context of state-supported terror and "surrogate terror," see J. Patrice McSherry, "Operation Condor: Clandestine Inter-American System," *Social Justice*, Winter 1999, accessible online. See also McSherry's concise summary article "Operation Condor: Cross-Border Disappearance and Death," TeleSUR, May 25, 2015, on the TeleSUR website (telesurtv.net). This includes an excellent map of South America with a country-by-country breakdown of some fifty thousand people "estimated to have been killed or 'disappeared'" by Operation Condor. The great majority of these atrocities took place in Argentina and Chile. McSherry is the author of *Predatory States: Operation Condor and Covert War in Latin America* (Rowman and Littlefield, 2005). For an acclaimed investigative account of US complicity in and cover up of one of the most notorious "dirty war" massacres that took place in El Salvador, see Mark Danner, *The Massacre at El Mozote: A Parable of the Cold War* (Vintage/Random House, 1994).

5   The Spanish-language SOA manuals discussed in the text are all accessible through the School of the Americas Watch website (soaw.org). For a critical summary of the manuals, with numerous translated quotations, see Latin American Working Group, "Declassified Army and CIA Manuals," at the lawg.org website. Some of the quotations introduced here and later in the text come from the latter source. The "cause of the poor" quotation appears in Gail Lumet Buckley, "Left, Right and Center,"

America, May 9, 1998.

6   *Psychological Operations in Guerrilla Warfare*, translated for the Contras under the title *Operaciones sicologicas en guerra de guerrillas*, can be accessed through the CIA website or, as used here, a version uploaded at fas.org. Evan Thomas, "How to 'Neutralize' the Enemy," *Time*, October 29, 1984.

7   The cartoon-style booklet *Manual del combatiente por la libertad* (*The Freedom Fighter's Manual* in English references) is accessible at several websites, including versions with English translation.

8   These resources can be accessed in full or in summary online at the following websites:

1.   For the declassified CIA manuals—*KUBARK Counterintelligence Interrogation* (July 1963) and *Human Resources Exploitation Training Manual—1983*—see the May 2014 National Security Archive (nsarchive.gwu.edu) release titled "Prisoner Abuse: Patterns from the Past." This includes a version of the *KUBARK* manual released in 2014 that still contains CIA redactions but is less sanitized than an earlier version declassified in 1997.

2.   The National Security Archive release also includes two short declassified entries pertinent to the seven SOA "torture manuals." One of these, from 1991, records a conversation with Major Victor Tise, who taught at the SOA from 1982 and prepared the so-called terror manuals. See "Document 4: DOD, USSOUTHCOM CI Training—Supplemental Information, CONFIDENTIAL, 31 July, 1991." Tise notes that the Carter administration had halted counterintelligence training courses "for fear training would contribute to Human Rights violations in other countries."

3.   All seven of the Spanish-language SOA manuals can be accessed via "SOA Manuals Index" at soaw.org.

4.   The two CIA and seven SOA manuals are analyzed and quoted at length in Latin America Working Group, "Declassified Army and CIA Manuals," lawg.org.

5.   Other extended analyses include Linda Haugaard, "Textbook Repression: US Training Manuals Declassified," c. 1997, at mediafilter.org.

6.   "Report on the School of the Americas," March 6, 1997, at

the Federation of American Scientists website (fas.org).

7. The *Washington Post* reported the seven SOA manuals had been distributed to "thousands" of officers in eleven countries. Dana Priest, "U.S. Instructed Latins on Executions, Torture," *Washington Post*, September 21, 1996.

9 These "public diplomacy" quotes come from various sources. For a sample, see the Defense Department's formal response to the issue when the SOA manuals first came under review in 1991 and 1992: "Fact Sheet Concerning Training Manuals Containing Materials Inconsistent with U.S. Policy," reprinted in National Security Archive, "Prisoner Abuse." See also Kepner, "Torture 101."

10 Barbara Jentzsch, "School of the Americas Critic," *Progressive*, July 1, 1992.

11 I address the mobilization of social science expertise as applied to "national character" studies of the Japanese in World War II in *War Without Mercy: Race and Power in the Pacific War* (Pantheon, 1986). For an excellent analysis that places the manuals in historical context, looking to both the past and future, see James Hodge and Linda Cooper, "Roots of Abu Ghraib in CIA Techniques," *National Catholic Reporter*, November 5, 2004.

12 McSweeny, "Operation Condor"; Kepner, "Torture 101."

13 Coatsworth, "The Cold War in Central America," 216–21.

Chapter 6: New and Old World Orders: The 1990s

1 Frank N. Schubert and Theresa L. Kraus, ed., *The Whirlwind War: The United States Army in Operations DESERT SHIELD and DESERT STORM* (Center of Military History, United States Army, 1995).

2 In the words of Anthony H. Cordesman, an influential American strategic commentator, writing before September 11, "The Gulf War reshaped the face of modern warfare. It demonstrated a dramatic increase in the importance of joint operations, high-paced air and armored operations, precision strike systems, night and all-weather warfare capabilities, sophisticated electronic warfare and command and control capabilities, and the ability to target and strike deep

behind the front line, marking what might be the beginning of a revolution in military affairs." See his "The Persian Gulf War" in John Whiteclay Chambers II, ed., *The Oxford Companion to American Military History* (Oxford University Press, 2000).

3   For a detailed official analysis (296 pages) that emphasizes the mesh of conventional practices and technological innovations in the air war that dominated operations, see Thomas A. Keaney and Eliot A. Cohen, *Gulf War Air Power Survey: Summary Report* (Historical Studies Division, Department of the Air Force, 1993), especially chapter 10 ("Was Desert Storm a Revolution in Warfare?"), 235–51; accessible online.

4   Michael G. Vickers and Robert C. Martinage, *The Revolution in War* (Center for Strategic and Budgetary Assessments, December 2004). This lengthy (227 pages) report provides an excellent technical overview of the revolution in military affairs. The quotes in this paragraph appear in the opening "Executive Summary." For a reevaluation from the same think tank, see Barry D. Watts, *The Maturing Revolution in Military Affairs* (Center for Strategic and Budgetary Assessments, 2011).

5   For coalition aircraft losses, see Department of Defense, "The Operation Desert Shield/Desert Storm Timeline," August 8, 2000; accessible at the DoD website (defense.gov). Estimates of Iraqi equipment destroyed in the "100-hour" ground war vary, but all agree that the destruction was massive. Cordesman in "The Persian Gulf War" puts it at roughly 3,200 Iraqi tanks, more than 900 other armored vehicles, and over 2,000 pieces of artillery.

6   Eric Rouleau, "The View from France: America's Unyielding Policy toward Iraq," *Foreign Affairs* 74, no. 1 (January/February 1995): 61–62.

7   Keaney and Cohen, *Gulf War Air Power Survey*, especially pages 46, 69, 71–77, 118–19, 218–21, 248–51; the "bloodlessness" comment appears on page 250.

8   US fatality estimates vary very slightly depending on the source.

9   Beth Osborne Daponte, "A Case Study in Estimating Casualties from War and Its Aftermath: the 1991 Persian Gulf War," *PSR Quarterly* (June 1993): 57–66; accessible online. Daponte, who served as a government demographer during the war, was interviewed by reporters in 2003 when the United States again

invaded Iraq. See "Toting the Casualties of War," *Businessweek,* February 5, 2003; also Jack Kelly, "Estimates of deaths in first war still in dispute," *Pittsburgh Post-Gazette,* February 16, 2003, accessible at the old.post-gazette.com website. When the Gulf War was followed by more than a decade of economic sanctions against Iraq, the issue of excessive morbidity (especially infant mortality) became a great source of controversy. This is discussed and annotated in John W. Dower, *Cultures of War: Pearl Harbor / Hiroshima / 9-11 / Iraq* (Norton and New Press, 2010), 90–93.

10   *War in the Persian Gulf: Operations Desert Shield and Desert Storm, August 1990–1991* (Center of Military History, U.S. Army, 2010); the quotes appear on pages v and 1.

11   *Public Papers of the Presidents of the United States: George H. W. Bush, 1991* (Government Printing Office, 1992), 197, 207.

12   Bush's speeches of September 11, 1990, and January 16 and 29, 1991, are accessible through various websites that provide comprehensive access to the public papers of US presidents. These include "Public Papers of the Presidents" made accessible through the National Archives (archives.gov), and presidency.ucsb.edu.

13   These paragraphs on the rhetoric of the 1990s "revolution in military affairs" draw on a range of online sources, including the following: General Accounting Office, *Joint Military Operations: Weaknesses in DOD's Process for Certifying C4I Systems Interoperability* (March 1998); Vickers and Martinage, *The Revolution in War*; Watts, *The Maturing Revolution in Military Affairs*; U.S. Navy, *Copernicus—Forward: C4I for the 21st Century* (June 1995), accessible at fas.org; Defense Technical Information Center, *C4I for the Warrior—Global Command & Control System: From Concept to Reality* (1996), accessible on the dtic.mil website; Admiral William A. Owens, "The Emerging U.S. System-of-Systems," Institute for National Strategic Studies, National Defense University, *Strategic Forum*, no. 63 (February 1996), also on dtic.mil; Vice Admiral Arthur K. Cebrowski and John J. Garstka, "Network-Centric Warfare: Its Origin and Future," *U.S. Naval Institute Proceedings,* January 1998, accessible on the usni.org website; William H. J. Manthorpe Jr., "The Emerging Joint System of Systems: Engineering Challenge and Opportunity for APL," *Johns Hopkins APL Technical Digest* 17, no. 3 (1996) [APL is the

acronym for Advanced Physics Laboratory], accessible on the jhuapl.edu website; Central Security Service, National Security Agency, *Maritime SIGINT Architecture Technical Standards Handbook, Version 1.0: Maritime Information Dominance for America* (March 1999), accessible at tscm.com.

14   Both JCS documents are readily accessible online. In *Joint Vision 2010: America's Military—Preparing for Tomorrow*, see especially pages 2, 11–14, 25–28. The quotation here appears on page 6 in *Joint Vision 2020*.

15   Manthorpe, "Emerging Joint System of Systems"; Owens, "Emerging U.S. System-of-Systems."

16   For an annotated commentary that taps this alarmist military and trade-publication literature, see the following unclassified paper submitted to the Marine Corps Command and Staff Col lege in 1996: Major Charles L. Hudson, "Remaining Relevant in the 21st Century" (Defense Technical Information Center), accessible on the dtic.mil website.

17   John A. Tures, "United States Military Operations in the New World Order," *American Diplomacy*, April 2003. According to Tures, 48 percent of the military operations after the Cold War ended received the approval of the United Nations, and 28 percent were done in conjunction with NATO (often overlapping with UN endorsement).

18   Andrew J. Bacevich, "Even If We Defeat the Islamic State, We'll Still Lose the Bigger War," *Washington Post*, October 3, 2014.

19   Chalmers Johnson, "America's Empire of Bases," online at *TomDispatch*, January 15, 2004. Johnson's Pentagon estimate was taken from the Department of Defense's *Base Structure Report* for fiscal year 2003. This article summarizes the argument he developed in *The Sorrows of Empire: Militarism, Secrecy, and the End of the Republic* (Metropolitan Books, 2004).

20   Basic navy publications emphasizing the new "littoral" mission include the following: . . . *From the Sea: Preparing the Naval Service for the 21st Century*, a September 1992 white paper accessible on the au.af.mil website; *Forward . . . from the Sea*, 1994, accessible on the dtic.mil website; and *Forward . . . from the Sea: The Navy Operational Concept*, March 1997, accessible on the navy.mil website. In the marine corps, General Myatt's "chaos in

the littorals" formulation helped lay the groundwork for Operation Urban Warrior, a training program introduced by the corps' Warfighting Laboratory in 1997. This focused on fighting in the "urban littoral" (also called the "concrete jungle"), where complex political, social, religious, and tribal strife could be anticipated. (The Urban Warrior logo is a ferocious sea monster looming over a populated coastline.) A 1990s study by a marine officer suggests that "the littoral" was understood to cover land areas "within 200 miles of the sea"; Hudson, "Remaining Relevant."

21   The "no-fly zone" operation, code-named Operation Southern Watch, fell under US Central Command and dispatched upwards of 150,000 flights over Iraq between 1992 and 2001. Around five thousand US troops were stationed in Saudi Arabia. Bin Laden, a native of Saudi Arabia, expressed his rage against the blasphemy of garrisoning US troops there on various occasions, most famously in a long fatwa delivered in 1996. "The latest and greatest of these aggressions, incurred by the Muslims since the death of the Prophet," he declared, "is the occupation of the land of the two Holy Places [Mecca and Medina]—the foundation of the house of Islam." This is accessible online at pbs.org among other websites.

Chapter 7: September 11 and "A New Kind of War"

1   The "worldwide attack matrix," well known in the journalistic literature on September 11, was first disclosed by Bob Woodward and Dan Balz in "At Camp David, Advise and Dissent," *Washington Post*, January 31, 2002. For Rumsfeld, see "America Widens 'Crusade' on Terror," online at BBC News, September 16, 2001. Cheney's famous "dark side" comment was made in a television interview on NBC on September 16, 2001.

2   Louise Richardson, *What Terrorists Want: Understanding the Enemy, Containing the Threat* (Random House, 2006), 167. In 2011, Lady Eliza Manningham-Buller, the former director general of MI5, the United Kingdom's national security intelligence agency, expressed similar sentiment by characterizing the September 11 attacks as "a crime, not an act of war," and declaring she "never

felt it helpful to refer to a war on terror." Terrorist campaigns, she said, could never be solved militarily; Richard Norton-Taylor, "MI5 Former Chief Decries 'War on Terror,'" *Guardian*, September 1, 2011.

3   In the early stages of the conflict—from September 11 through the invasions of Afghanistan and Iraq until around 2004, when it became clear the war on terror had become a quagmire—top officials evoked World War II with a spectrum of false analogies they appear to have sincerely believed appropriate. "Weapons of mass destruction" held a central place in this, reinforced by choreographed allusions to the specter of a "mushroom cloud." President Bush conjured the Axis enemy of World War II by famously declaring that the real global threat was an "axis of evil" composed of Iraq, Iran, and North Korea. The invasion of Iraq was accompanied by comparisons to the post-1945 Allied occupations of Germany and Japan. The disastrous purge of Sunni and Baathist officers and bureaucrats in occupied Iraq, which effectively wiped out governance and seeded the future insurgency, was explicitly modeled on the "de-Nazification" program in occupied Germany. On May 1, 2003, when President Bush prematurely declared victory in Iraq under a banner reading "Mission Accomplished," his stage directors set the scene on an aircraft carrier off the coast of California in undisguised mimicry of General Douglas MacArthur taking the Japanese surrender on the battleship *Missouri* in Tokyo Bay in September 1945.

4   The "cakewalk" idiom came from Ken Adelman, a neoconservative member of the advisory Defense Policy Board; see his op-ed pieces in the *Washington Post* on February 13, 2002 ("Cakewalk in Iraq") and April 10, 2003 ("'Cakewalk' Revisited").

5   Donald Rumsfeld, "A New Kind of War," *New York Times*, September 27, 2001. John Esterbrook, "Rumsfeld: It Would Be a Short War," CBS News, November 15, 2002, on the cbsnews.com website.

6   For a sample of the vast critical commentary on Rumsfeld and the Iraq War fiasco, see Mark Danner's review article "Rumsfeld: Why We Live in His Ruins," *New York Review of Books*, February 6, 2014. The review addresses Errol Morris's interview

documentary *The Unknown Known*, Rumsfeld's memoir *Known and Unknown: A Memoir*, and Bradley Graham, *By His Own Rules: The Ambitions, Successes, and Ultimate Failures of Donald Rumsfeld.*

7   The full text of *The Management of Savagery* translated by William McCants is available online. Scholars like Scott Atran, Malise Ruthven, and Jason Burke have been insightful in challenging "clash of civilizations" approaches to Islamist terrorism and calling attention to the secular, "rational," managerial, and sociological—as well as irrational, dogmatic, and atrocious— strains in global terrorism.

8   Anthony H. Cordesman, "The Real Revolution in Military Affairs," Center for Strategic and International Studies, 2014, accessible on the csis.org website.

9   Tim Shorrock, "The Corporate Takeover of U.S. Intelligence," *Salon*, June 1, 2007, accessible on the salon.com website. Dana Priest and William M. Arkin, "Top Secret America: A Hidden World, Growing Beyond Control," *Washington Post*, July 19, 2010. This investigative report, including charts and other graphics, is accessible at washingtonpost.com/topsecretamerica.

10   See the table in Ulrich Petersohn, "Privatizing Security: The Limits of Military Outsourcing," *CSS Analysis in Security Policy* (Center for Security Studies, ETH Zurich, September 2010), accessible on the css.ethz.ch website.

11   Esther Pan, "Iraq: Military Outsourcing," Council on Foreign Relations, May 20, 2004, accessible on the cfr.org website. For data, see the following two Congressional Research Service reports: Moshe Schwarz and Joyprada Swain, "Department of Defense Contractors in Afghanistan and Iraq: Background and Analysis," May 13, 2011; Heidi M. Peters, Moshe Schwartz, and Lawrence Kapp, "Department of Defense Contractor and Troop Levels in Iraq and Afghanistan: 2007–2016," August 15, 2016. The literature on privatization of military services is enormous.

12   For an influential early exposé of "extraordinary rendition," see Jane Mayer, "Outsourcing Torture: The Secret History of America's 'Extraordinary Rendition' Program," *New Yorker*, February 14, 2005. For a detailed (216 pages) later analysis, see Open Society Justice Initiative, *Globalizing Torture: CIA Secret*

Detention and Extraordinary Rendition (Open Society Foundations, 2013), accessible on the opensocietyfoundations.org website. This report identifies fifty-four nations that colluded with the CIA in this secret operation and identifies 136 individuals who were interrogated.

13   David M. Herszenhorn, "Estimates of Iraq War Cost Were Not Close to Ballpark," *New York Times*, March 19, 2008. President Bush's chief economic adviser Lawrence B. Lindsey was criticized for telling the *Wall Street Journal* in September 2002 that war costs might run higher than others were saying. Rumsfeld, for one, belittled this and said the budget office had come up with "a number that's something under $50 billion." For Rumsfeld and other early war-cost underestimates, see Martin Wolk, "Cost of Iraq War Could Surpass $1 Trillion," NBC News, March 17, 2006, accessible at nbcnews.com.

14   Linda J. Bilmes, "The Financial Legacy of Iraq and Afghanistan: How Wartime Spending Decisions Will Constrain Future National Security Budgets," March 2013, Harvard Kennedy School Research Working Paper (RWP13-006), accessible at hks.harvard.edu. For a complementary detailed analysis of the usually hidden costs of these wars, see Neta C. Crawford, "U.S. Costs of War Through 2014: $4.4 Trillion and Counting," June 25, 2014, uploaded on Brown University's Watson Institute for International and Public Affairs website at watson.brown.edu. Both of these reports are densely annotated. They are also introduced, along with the conservative bookkeeping of the Congressional Budget Office and Congressional Research Service, in Anthony H. Cordesman, *The FY2016 Defense Budget and US Strategy: Key Trends and Data Points* (Center for Strategic and International Studies, March 2, 2015), 45–52. One often-cited conventional analysis of appropriated war costs is Amy Belasco, "The Cost of Iraq, Afghanistan, and Other Global War on Terror Operations Since 9/11" (Congressional Research Service Report RL33110, December 8, 2014), accessible at fas.org.

15   Watson Institute for International and Public Affairs, Brown University, "US & Allied Killed," Costs of War website, updated February 2015; also "The Costs of War Since 2001: Iraq, Afghanistan, and Pakistan," updated April 2015. As of January 2016, the Iraq

Body Count website placed total violent deaths in Iraq including combatants at 251,000. Its database of over 47,000 "documented" cases beginning in January 2003 put civilian deaths from the violence between 160,033 and 178,849. On population displacements, see the itemized "Annex Table 1" in UNHCR, *Global Trends: Forced Displacement in 2015*, 57–60.

16   *Body Count: Casualty Figures after 10 Years of the "War on Terror"—Iraq, Afghanistan, Pakistan*, 1st international edition, March 2015. The collaborating organizations that issued this report are the International Physicians for the Prevention of Nuclear War (Germany), Physicians for Social Responsibility (United States), and Physicians for Global Survival (Canada). This is accessible at the Physicians for Social Responsibility website (psr.org). The report is based on an October 2014 version prepared by the German group. There are, of course, lower estimates as well; the Wikipedia entry for "War on Terror" cites and annotates a great range of "casualties" estimates for Iraq and Afghanistan.

17   Watson Institute for International and Public Affairs, Brown University, "US Veterans & Military Families," Costs of War website, updated January 2015. On very recent research on traumatic brain injury, see Alan Schwarz, "Research Traces Link Between Combat Blasts and PTSD," *New York Times*, June 9, 2016; also Robert F. Worth, "What If PTSD Is More Physical Than Psychological?" *New York Times*, June 10, 2016.

18   National Center for PTSD, "How Common Is PTSD?" (Department of Veterans Affairs, n.d.), accessible on the ptsd.va.gov website (for percentage estimates of PTSD incidence in the Vietnam, Gulf, Iraq, and Afghanistan wars). A 2015 government study includes a table itemizing 327,299 "Traumatic Brain Injury Incidents" between 2000 and early 2015, the great majority of which were categorized as "mild": Hannah Fischer, *A Guide to U.S. Military Casualty Statistics: Operation Freedom's Sentinel, Operation Inherent Resolve, Operation New Dawn, Operation Iraqi Freedom, and Operation Enduring Freedom* (Congressional Research Study, August 7, 2015), 4. See also PTSD and TBI data in chapter 1 above.

19   Bilmes, "The Financial Legacy of Iraq and Afghanistan," 4–9.

20   The short Gulf War also has a pervasive but poorly understood
      and treated legacy of disability called Gulf War Syndrome. The
      Veterans Administration describes this as "a cluster of medically
      unexplained chronic symptoms that can include fatigue, head-
      aches, joint pain, indigestion, insomnia, dizziness, respiratory
      disorders, and memory problems." Suggested possible causes
      include exposure to oil-well fires, burn pits, pesticides, vaccines,
      or other chemicals.

21   President Bush often spoke of the war on terror in these terms.
      See his "Remarks to the National Endowment for Democracy,"
      October 6, 2005 ("this fight resembles the struggle against
      Communism") accessed at georgewbush-whitehouse.archives;
      also "Remarks on the Anniversary of Operation Iraqi Freedom,"
      March 19, 2004, accessed through US Government Publishing
      Office at gpo.gov ("There is no neutral ground—no neutral
      ground—in the fight between civilization and terror, because
      there is no neutral ground between good and evil, freedom and
      slavery, and life and death").

22   The 2003 documentary film is Errol Morris's prize-winning *The
      Fog of War: Eleven Lessons from the Life of Robert S. McNamara*;
      an online transcript is accessible on the errolmorris.com website.
      In this interview, McNamara also discusses his participation as
      a young systems analyst in the saturation bombing of Japan in
      1945 and indicates that he now regarded this as a war crime.

23   Department of the Army, *Counterinsurgency* (FM 3-24), December
      2006; the same 282-page field manual was issued to the marine
      corps (MCWP 3-33.5). This unclassified text is accessible online.

24   Failing to learn from the Soviet defeat in Afghanistan, neglecting
      counterinsurgency, and ignoring middle-echelon military and
      civilian warnings about invading Iraq are discussed in Dower,
      Cultures of War, 127–32. Where top-level dismissal of unwel-
      come information is concerned, the lengthy "Chilcot report"
      (*The Report of the Iraq Inquiry*) released in England in July 2016
      similarly concluded that "The risks of internal strife in Iraq,
      active Iranian pursuit of its interests, regional instability, and Al
      Qaida activity in Iraq, were each explicitly identified before the
      invasion" but ignored by Prime Minister Tony Blair and his top
      policymakers. See the July 6, 2016, statement by Sir John Chilcot

on the occasion of the issuance of the report, at the inquiry's website (iraqinquiry.org.uk); also Jonathan Steele, "Trouble at the FCO," *London Review of Books*, July 28, 2016.

25   General Jack Keane in a televised interview on *NewsHour with Jack Lehrer*, April 18, 2006. John A. Nagel quotes this in his foreword to the new *Counterinsurgency* manual, xiii–xv.

Chapter 8: Arcs of Instability

1   Japan as the last domino is addressed in John W. Dower, "The Superdomino in Postwar Asia: Japan In and Out of the Pentagon Papers," in Noam Chomsky and Howard Zinn, ed., *The Pentagon Papers: The Senator Gravel Edition*, vol. 5 (Beacon Press, 1972), 101–42.

2   National Intelligence Council, *Mapping the Global Future: Report of the National Intelligence Council's 2020 Project* (December 2004), 97, 117, 118.

3   Many recent critical writings reinforce this point. See, for a sample, Patrick Cockburn, "The Age of Disintegration: Neoliberalism, Interventionism, the Resource Curse, and a Fragmenting World," *TomDispatch*, June 28, 2016.

4   Karen DeYoung and Greg Jaffe, "U.S. 'Secret War' Expands Globally as Special Operations Forces Take Larger Role," *Washington Post*, June 4, 2010 ("seventy-five countries"). For "150 countries," see Claudette Roulo, "Votel Takes Charge of Special Operations Command," *DoD News*, on the defense.gov website. The investigative journalist Nick Turse, writing on the website *TomDispatch*, is the most incisive critical observer of such overt and covert US operations during the Obama administration. See his "A Secret War in 120 Countries" (August 3, 2011); "Obama's Arc of Instability" (September 18, 2011); "The Special Ops Surge: America's Secret War in 134 Countries" (January 16, 2014); "The Golden Age of Black Ops" (January 20, 2015); and "Iraq, Afghanistan, and Other Special Ops 'Successes'" (October 25, 2015).

5   John Sifton, "A Brief History of Drones," *Nation*, February 27, 2012, is insightful on the early origins, nomenclature, and complex psychology of high-tech targeted killings.

6   On the "tall man" operation, see Sifton, "A Brief History of
     Drones." Regularly updated data on drone strikes in Pakistan,
     Yemen, and Somalia is posted by the British online site Bureau of
     Investigative Journalism (thebureauinvestigates.com).

7   Scott Shane, "Drone Strikes Reveal Uncomfortable Truth: U.S.
     Is Often Unsure About Who Will Die," *New York Times*, April
     23, 2015 (for numbers); Tom Engelhardt, "Who Counts: Body
     Counts, Drones, and 'Collateral Damage' (aka 'Bug Splat')," *Tom-
     Dispatch*, May 3, 2015 (for phrases).

8   Jay Solomon and Carol E. Lee, "Obama Contends with Arc of
     Instability Unseen Since '70s," *Wall Street Journal*, July 13, 2014.

9   Andrew F. Krepinevich, *The Quadrennial Defense Review:
     Rethinking the US Military Posture* (Center for Strategic and Bud-
     getary Assessments, October 24, 2005), 4; see also Krepinevich's
     testimony on "The Quadrennial Defense Review" (a government
     strategic assessment) before the Committee on Armed Services,
     US House of Representatives, September 14, 2005. Krepinevich's
     influential reports can be accessed through the Center for Strate-
     gic and Budgetary Assessments (CSBA) website csbaonline.org.
     The CSBA is an independent strategic think tank with close ties
     to the US government and military.

10   Hans Kristensen, *Nuclear Futures: Proliferation of Weapons of
     Mass Destruction and US Nuclear Strategy* ("Basic Research Re-
     port 98.2," British American Security Information Council, March
     1998), accessible on the nukestrat.com website. This densely an-
     notated report provides a close analysis of the repurposing of the
     nuclear mission, including internal debate in Pentagon circles. See
     also Kristensen's "Targets of Opportunity," *Bulletin of the Atomic
     Scientists* (September/October 1997): 22–28.

11   Kristensen, *Nuclear Futures*, 12, 17, 20, 21 (collateral damage);
     19–20 (mini-nukes); 22 ("weapon rich environment").

12   Policy Subcommittee, Strategic Advisory Group, US Strategic
     Command, "Essentials of Post-Cold War Deterrence" (1995).
     The original typed eight-page memo is accessible on the nuke-
     strat.com website. The "weapons of mass destruction" referred
     to included chemical and biological weapons, which the United
     States itself had previously renounced using.

13   See, for example, entries on START I on the websites of the Arms

Control Association (armscontrol.org), Nuclear Threat Initiative (nti.org), and Federation of American Scientists (fas.org).

14   These figures derive from tables in the "Nuclear Weapons" section of the Johnston's Archive website at johnstonsarchive.net.

15   The 2002 *Nuclear Posture Review* was classified, but extensive excerpts were made available to Congress on December 31, 2001, and are accessible on the globalsecurity.org website. For policy toward China, see Kristensen, Norris, and McKenzie, *Chinese Nuclear Forces and U.S. Nuclear Policy.*

16   Hans Kristensen has prepared two document-driven timelines of these plans and reports: "The Role of Nuclear Weapons in Regional Counterproliferation and Global Strike Scenarios," University of New Mexico workshop, September 2008 (from which the "global strike" quotations in this paragraph are taken), accessible on the fas.org website; "U.S. Nuclear Weapons Guidance," Nuclear Information Project, 2008; accessible on the nukestrat.com website.

17   For a brief summary of US engagement with nuclear treaties, which is not addressed here, see Jonathan E. Medalia, *Comprehensive Nuclear Test-Ban Treaty: Background and Current Developments* (Congressional Research Service, September 29, 2014), 2–3, accessible on the fas.org website.

18   The quotes here are from the first two of the five jointly authored *Wall Street Journal* articles: "A World Free of Nuclear Weapons" (January 4, 2007) and "Toward a Nuclear-Free World" (January 15, 2008).

19   "Message from the President on the New START Treaty," February 2, 2011.

20   For the official March 2015 figures, see Arms Control Association, "Nuclear Weapons: Who Has What at a Glance," April 2015, on the armscontrol.org website. For slightly higher 2015 data, with illuminating critical commentary, see Federation of American Scientists, "Status of World Nuclear Forces," April 28, 2015 update, on the fas.org website.

21   William J. Broad and David E. Sanger, "U.S. Ramping Up Major Renewal in Nuclear Arms," *New York Times*, September 22, 2014.

22   Federation of American Scientists, "Status of World Nuclear Forces."

23   "The New Nuclear Age: Why the Risks of Conflict Are Rising,"
        Economist, March 7–13, 2015; see also "Still on the Eve of De-
        struction," *Economist*, November 20, 2014 (special issue on "The
        World in 2015").

24   Carnegie Endowment, *Universal Compliance: A Strategy for
        Nuclear Security*, tables 4.2 and 4.4 (uranium and plutonium
        figures). Graham Allison has addressed the possibility of nuclear
        terrorism in various places. See "A Response to Nuclear Terrorism
        Skeptics," *Brown University Journal of World Affairs* (Fall/Winter
        2009): 31–44; also "Nuclear Terrorism Fact Sheet," Belfer Center
        for Science and International Affairs, Harvard Kennedy School,
        April 2010, accessible through belfercenter.ksg.harvard.edu.

Chapter 9: The American Century at Seventy-Five

1   For arms sales, see Catherine A. Theohary, *Conventional Arms
        Transfers to Developing Nations, 2007–2014* (Congressional Re-
        search Service, December 21, 2015), especially the pie charts for
        2007–10 and 2011–14 on page 20.

2   There is a certain sorcery of names involved in declaring the
        end of wars that do not actually end. Officially, the US war in
        Afghanistan was called Operation Enduring Freedom and ran
        from October 7, 2001, to December 28, 2014. Effective January
        1, 2015, the new mission in Afghanistan was called Operation
        Freedom's Sentinel (which in turn was a component, with NATO
        forces, of Operation Resolute Support). The war in Iraq, called
        Operation Iraqi Freedom, ran from March 19, 2003, to August
        31, 2010, on which date President Obama announced the end
        of the US combat mission. Effective September 1, 2010, the
        military operation in Iraq was called Operation New Dawn. On
        December 31, 2011, the war in Iraq was declared officially ended.
        For a timeline, see Barbara Salazar Torreon, "U.S. Periods of War
        and Dates of Recent Conflicts" (Congressional Research Service,
        February 27, 2015). President Obama's attempt to retire the
        GWOT terminology came in a speech at the National Defense
        University on May 23, 2013, in which he stated, "We must define
        our effort not as a boundless 'global war on terror'—but rather

as a series of persistent, targeted efforts to dismantle specific networks of violent extremists that threaten America." The full text is accessible at the White House website (whitehouse.gov).

3   "War in Afghanistan: The General's Words," *Economist*, June 11, 2016; Peters, Schwartz, and Kapp, "Department of Defense Contractor and Troop Levels in Iraq and Afghanistan"; Tom Vanden Brook, "New Rules Allow More Civilian Casualties in Air War against ISIS," *Military Times*, April 19, 2016 ("forty thousand bombs").

4   The full Chilcot report, consisting of a 150-page executive summary, twelve volumes of documentation, and a statement by Sir John Chilcot, chair of the inquiry, on July 6, 2016, when the report was issued, is accessible at iraqinquiry.org.uk. The inquiry assesses UK policy on Iraq from 2001 to 2009. It does not, however, address the issue of the legality of the invasion of Iraq. On this, see, for example, Philippe Sands, "A Grand and Disastrous Deceit," *London Review of Books*, July 28, 2016; also Richard Falk, "Is Genocide a Controversial International Crime?," July 30, 2016, accessed at richardfalk.wordpress.com on the Global Justice in the 21st Century website.

Index

About Dispatch Books

After nearly a decade working together at *TomDispatch.com*, publishing some of the most thoughtful, powerful, and prescient writers of the post-9/11 era, legendary book editor Tom Engelhardt and award-winning journalist Nick Turse founded Dispatch Books in 2012.

Joining with Haymarket Books, the independent imprint has forged a storied history in a short amount of time, producing important, award-winning works of fiction and nonfiction. From Pulitzer Prize–winner John Dower's searing indictment of US military power since World War II, *The Violent American Century*, and Ann Jones's up-close-and-personal look at the toll of recent wars on America's veterans, *They Were Soldiers*, to John Feffer's breakout dystopian thriller *Splinterlands* and Nick Turse's American Book Award–winning exposé of US military operations in Africa, *Tomorrow's Battlefield*, Dispatch Books has quickly distinguished itself as a home for influential authors and one of the premier imprints in progressive publishing.

About Haymarket Books

Haymarket Books is a nonprofit, progressive book distributor and publisher, a project of the Center for Economic Research and Social Change. We believe that activists need to take ideas, history, and politics into the many struggles for social justice today. Learning the lessons of past victories, as well as defeats, can arm a new generation of fighters for a better world. For more information and to shop our complete catalog of titles, visit us online at www.haymarketbooks.org.

About the Author

Photo by Ken Dower

JOHN W. DOWER is professor emeritus of history at the Massachusetts Institute of Technology. His many books include *War Without Mercy: Race and Power in the Pacific War* and *Embracing Defeat: Japan in the Wake of World War Two*, which won numerous prizes including the Pulitzer and the National Book Award.